OTAKU FOOD!

OTAKU FOOD!

JAPANESE SOUL FOOD INSPIRED BY ANIME AND POP CULTURE

DANIELLE BAGHERNEJAD

TURNER
PUBLISHING COMPANY

Turner Publishing Company
Nashville, Tennessee
www.turnerpublishing.com

Food photography and styling: © Danielle Baghernejad
Cover and Art Direction: Jermaine Lau

Otaku Food!: Japanese Soul Food Inspired by Anime and Pop Culture

Library of Congress Cataloging-in-Publication number: 2020934377
ISBN: (print) 978-1-64250-333-3

BISAC: CKB048000—COOKING / Regional & Ethnic / Japanese

Printed in the United States of America

For my husband, Eamon, you're my inspiration.

TABLE OF CONTENTS

HISTORICAL

WHAT'S IN A NAME...

Otaku (おたく), **literally translated as "your house", is a Japanese slang word for nerd. As in, you're such a nerd—you never leave your house since you're so busy obsessing over your hobby. A little harsh, right?**

In Japan, being an otaku sometimes means you're someone with extreme, obsessive interests, usually with anime, manga, or games. While it can been seen in a negative light there, in America, otaku is quite the opposite: many otaku wear their label with pride! Attend an anime convention and you'll see, otaku are a proud, fun, and amazing group of people!

But the term otaku doesn't have to be limited to just one category. I view myself as an anime otaku and so much more. A self-proclaimed "foodie," I consider myself a food otaku, going to extreme lengths to enjoy the best dishes this world has to offer. Food is my passion, and I love nothing more than sharing a good meal with good friends. Make it Japanese food, and we're in heaven!

Put it all together, and you get Otaku Food. This book is an otaku haven, filled to the brim with a love of anime, food, and all things Japan.

I hope you enjoy this nerdy culinary journey, and learn to embrace your inner otaku along the way!

YOUKOSO, FELLOW OTAKU!

So, what exactly is anime, and why write a cookbook about it?

For those of you seasoned veterans in the world of anime and manga, its comic book counterpart, the answer may seem obvious. But for those of you just starting to explore the wonders of otaku culture, you're in for a treat!

Let's start with the first question. Anime, or Japanese style animation, may seem like mere cartoons to the untrained eye, but after watching a few episodes, you'll start to notice something a little different. Anime is animated, yes, but it is very different than American style cartoons. What exactly makes it so special?

While they are written for a younger audience, the writers don't generally treat their intended audience as kids. Not afraid to deal with real stuff and unconcerned with sheltering kids from the complexities of life, anime stories are generally much deeper than a regular cartoon. Multi-episode story arcs portray complex characters dealing with some seriously heavy stuff: tragedy, happiness, loss, failure, self-discovery, silliness...basically, life. There are real characters dealing with real problems: it's relatable and draws you in. Not only that, but the stories themselves are generally written for a variety of viewers. When talking about demographics, there are five main categories:

- *Kodomomuke*, directed at young children, similar to American cartoons.
- *Shonen*, directed at younger boys, typically under sixteen.
- *Shojo*, directed at younger girls, typically under sixteen.
- *Seinen*, directed at older men, sixteen to thirty.
- *Josei*, directed at older women, typically sixteen to thirty.

You might expect the *kodomumuke* category to be the biggest, and it does have some long running series under its belt, but it's actually the least well known category abroad, the most popular series falling under the shonen or seinen domains. And while you might expect violence in seinen series, even younger audiences are not afraid to deal with mature topics in some form, and as a result create quite a cult following. For example, *One Piece* is one of the longest running shonen titles out there, yet quite a few mothers and college students watch it as well, all over the world! It is a show for kids, but it is by no means just a kids show.

That answers the first question. But why write a cookbook about it? That's easy. Since anime is filled with depth, the writers and animators add detail everywhere they can, even the food! They don't hold back when animating dishes, which results in truly mouthwatering scenes. Just imagine heaping bowls of fresh rice, with steam wafting slowly through the air while delectable toppings slowly cascade down the side. Even better, picture sizzling meat grilling on an open flame, juices dripping down and crackling on the hot coals, shining ever so lusciously as a sweet glaze is brushed on it's perfectly seared surface. The animators understand that the experience is in the details. It's no wonder so many people want to try the food!

There are plenty of cookbooks out there, but when it comes to Japanese food, it's rarer to find ones covering homestyle food. The food in anime isn't like the formal, fancier dishes seen in restaurants; no, those cookbooks are plentiful, and delicious, but don't quite hit the spot.

What is needed to understand anime is more soul food cooking—simple dishes made in real kitchens by everyday people, not chefs. I learned how to make homestyle Japanese food the

hard way, scouring the web, translating Japanese websites, buying numerous cookbooks during trips to Tokyo, and most importantly, experimenting at length in the kitchen, trying to understand just what makes the cuisine unique. While some of these recipes may be a little challenging, my goal was to make a cookbook sharing Japanese comfort food, with skills, recipes, and ingredients accessible to anyone.

Being a foodie at heart, I believe that to really understand a culture, you need to experience their relationship with food. We may not all speak the same language, but we all understand the language of food. Putting yourself in their shoes, experiencing the differences in how they enjoy the same ingredients in unique ways, or what unique ingredients are important to them—that is an experience that transcends language, and Japan's food is quite the experience to have!

Through these pages, I hope you find yourself transported to a new world, seeing your favorite anime in a new light after you've savored their characteristic dishes. Now, without further ado, *itadakimasu!* (Let's eat!)

JAPANESE PANTRY STAPLES

Most of these ingredients can be found in your local grocery store, but a handful you may have to find in an Asian grocery store. Most difficult-to-find ingredients are bottled or dried, by the way, so they are also available online! When in doubt, Amazon is a great source, so buy in bulk and stock up!

BAMBOO SHOOTS

The young shoots of the bamboo plant. Fresh bamboo shoots are a symbol of spring and only available for a short time, but canned bamboo shoots are available all year. They have a crisp, neutral taste that adds texture and interest to dishes.

BONITO FLAKES

The shavings from dried bonito fish, called katsuobushi in Japanese. Bonito flakes are a staple in Japanese kitchens, used as a topping to sprinkle on pretty much anything, as well as used to make dashi stock. Since it's dried, it keeps for a long time!

DAIKON RADISH

A large, round white root vegetable, with a crunchy texture. Daikon is a great addition to stir fries and stews, excellent for pickling, and also popular to grate and use as a condiment alongside meat dishes. It can be substituted with regular radishes for texture, but the daikon's flavor is more peppery.

DASHI

The quintessential soup stock used as a base for many dishes. Made from bonito flakes and seaweed, it can be made from scratch, but instant dashi granules are actually quite an excellent substitute and sold in little bottles. If fish isn't your thing, you can substitute chicken or vegetable broth. (See recipe.)

EDAMAME

The green, young soybeans. Both shelled and unshelled edamame are popular snacks, typically found in the freezer section. Sprinkled with sea salt they are excellent to munch on (especially while drinking!) but they can be added to many dishes for extra nutritional value.

FURIKAKE

A dry or semi dry condiment that is used to sprinkle on top of noodle and rice dishes. Commercial dishes typically contain sesame and seaweed, alongside a few other flavorings, but it's easy to make yourself! (See recipe.)

GINGER

Fresh ginger is used extensively in Japanese cuisine, never powdered ginger. Minced and grated, it adds subtle freshness to sauces and stir fries, and is a great addition to tea! Keep ginger wrapped in plastic wrap in the fridge in between use.

KOMBU SEAWEED

A thick, dark, leathery seaweed used mainly for making dashi. Bought dried, it snaps easily into smaller pieces, and a little goes a long way in terms of flavor. It's tough, chewy texture is also enjoyed on its own, eaten as pickled or stewed dish.

MIRIN

A sweet, fortified liquor used for cooking, never drinking. One of the core flavors in Japanese cooking, it's worth buying it online if you can't get your hands on it in person, but can be substituted with sweet sherry in recipes. Hon-mirin is naturally made mirin with about 20 percent alcohol content, whereas aji-mirin is an almost alcohol-free mirin substitute.

MISO

A salty soybean paste, it's often made with either wheat, rice, or barley mixed in and fermented for over a year for flavors to develop. Highly nutritious and delicious, it's used in a variety of dishes. The most versatile type of miso is white miso, which is actually a light brown color. It keeps forever in the fridge, so don't be afraid to buy a larger container.

NORI SEAWEED

A dried seaweed processed into paperlike sheets for sushi, it's the most common seaweed variety available outside Japan. Most often used as a wrapping or shredded up as a topping, it's paperlike texture falls apart when used in simmered or stewed dishes.

Store it in airtight packaging between use to keep the sheets crisp, and if it turns stale, hold a sheet over a stove burner for a few seconds until the color turns a little darker to revive the flavor.

RICE

The most common type of rice in Japan is medium grain rice, sometimes labeled as sushi rice. It has a unique, sticky texture that other types of rice cannot replicate, so especially for sushi and onigiri, getting your hands on good Japanese rice is essential. You can substitute other shorter-grain rice when you're in a pinch, but basmati, jasmine, wild, or other types of long grain rice just won't do.

RICE VINEGAR

A mild vinegar suitable for salad dressings and marinades, when mixed with sugar and a pinch of salt, it's used to season sushi rice. If you cannot find rice vinegar, use a white wine vinegar instead.

SAKE

The favorite of Japan, sake is an alcoholic beverage made from fermented rice. Sake is a key flavor for Japanese cuisine, used to downplay the gamey flavor of fish and meat. Since you're cooking with it, you don't need the fancy stuff, but if you can't find it, dry sherry can be used as a substitute.

SESAME OIL

Made from toasted sesame seeds, sesame oil has a rich, deep flavor. Better suited as a condiment instead of the main oil for cooking, it adds a great toasty flavor to dishes.

SESAME SEEDS

Both black and white sesame seeds are used in Japanese cooking, typically toasted and lightly crushed to bring out more of the nutty flavor trapped inside.

SHIITAKE MUSHROOMS

Available fresh or dried, I prefer using them dried since they keep forever and are easy to reconstitute with water. They have a denser texture, and the stems can be quite woody, so I typically use the tops for eating and the stems for making dashi.

SOBA NOODLES

Thin noodles made from buckwheat with a subtle, nutty flavor. The dried versions are easy to find, though fresh noodles are a delicious treat!

SOMEN NOODLES

Super thin noodles that cook very quickly, they are the Japanese version of angel hair pasta.

SOY SAUCE

A foundation ingredient of Japanese food, it comes in several varieties. Dark soy sauce is the most versatile, but light soy sauce has a sweeter, saltier flavor. Tamari soy sauce is a thicker version best suited as a dipping sauce. Try to find a Japanese brand, since the flavors can differ between Asian cuisines.

TOFU

Made from soybeans, two main types of tofu used in Japanese food are silken tofu and firm tofu. Firm tofu is more versatile and can be used in anything, whereas silken tofu is best enjoyed as is or in miso soup.

UDON NOODLES

Thick, chewy noodles that can be bought, these noodles are easy to make by hand! (See recipe.) Fresh udon has a denser texture than dried noodles, and they can sometimes be found in the frozen section.

WAKAME SEAWEED

A dark green seaweed that's used in salads, soups, and vinegared dishes, it's the classic seaweed in miso soup. Sold dried, a little goes a long way, so when reconstituting it, it will grow quite a few times in size.

THE ESSENTIAL SAUCES

There are a few basic sauces used in Japanese cooking, and they can be used as is as condiments or salad dressings. Since they're easy to make ahead, it's a good practice to have several sauces on hand in the fridge. When used as a marinade, vinegar based sauces are excellent for vegetables and chicken, while the thicker sauces are better for beef.

PONZU SAUCE

Makes 1 cup

Ingredients

- ½ cup soy sauce
- ¼ cup lemon juice
- ¼ cup orange juice
- 2 tablespoons mirin
- 1 tablespoon sugar

Combine all ingredients in a sealed container. Let sit for at least 30 minutes to let flavors combine. Refrigerate until ready to use.

VINEGAR SAUCE (SANBAIZU)

Makes 1 cup

Ingredients

- ⅔ cup rice vinegar
- 4 tablespoons sugar
- 3 tablespoon soy sauce

Combine all ingredients in a sealed container. Let sit for at least 30 minutes to let flavors combine. Refrigerate until ready to use.

TERIYAKI SAUCE

Makes 1 cup

Ingredients

- ½ cup soy sauce
- ¼ cup sake
- ¼ cup mirin
- ¼ cup brown sugar
- 1 clove garlic, minced

In a saucepan, combine all ingredients. Bring to a boil, then turn heat down to low. Let simmer 5 minutes for the alcohol to cook off, then remove from heat. Refrigerate until ready to use.

*To thicken the sauce, bring the liquid to a boil, then combine 1 tablespoon of cornstarch with a tablespoon of water to create a slurry, and mix into the sauce. Simmer for a few minutes until the sauce begins to thicken, then remove from heat.

YAKINIKU SAUCE

Makes 1 cup

Ingredients

- ¼ cup soy sauce
- 2 tablespoons sake
- 2 tablespoons mirin
- 1 tablespoon sugar
- 1 teaspoon rice vinegar
- ¼ fuji apple, grated
- 1 clove garlic, minced

In a saucepan, combine all ingredients. Bring to a boil, then turn heat down to low. Let simmer 5 minutes for the alcohol to cook off. Use a fine mesh strainer to strain out the apple pulp, pouring the sauce into a sealed container. Refrigerate until ready to use.

*To thicken the sauce, bring the strained liquid to a boil, then combine 1 tablespoon of cornstarch with a tablespoon of water to create a slurry, and mix into the sauce. Simmer for a few minutes until the sauce begins to thicken, then remove from heat.

SESAME SAUCE (GOMA DARE)

Makes ½ cup

Ingredients

- ¼ cup sake
- 2 tablespoons tahini (sesame paste)
- 1 tablespoon ponzu sauce
- 1 tablespoon miso
- 1 tablespoon sesame oil
- 1 clove garlic, minced

Combine all ingredients in a sealed container. Let sit for at least 30 minutes to let flavors combine. Refrigerate until ready to use.

TONKATSU SAUCE

Makes ½ cup

Ingredients

- ⅓ cup ketchup
- 2 tablespoons Worcestershire sauce
- 2 tablespoons soy sauce
- 1 tablespoon mirin
- 1 tablespoon sugar

Combine all ingredients in a small bowl. Let sit for at least 30 minutes to let flavors combine. Refrigerate until ready to use.

JAPANESE STYLE MAYONNAISE

Makes 1 cup

Ingredients

- 1 egg yolk, at room temperature
- ¾ cup vegetable oil
- 1 teaspoon Dijon mustard
- ¼ teaspoon salt
- 1 teaspoon sugar
- 1 tablespoon rice vinegar
- 1 tablespoon lemon juice

Add the egg yolk and mustard to a food processor or blender and process to combine. With the blades running, slowly drizzle half the oil into the blender in a slow and steady stream.

When the mixture has thickened, add the salt and sugar, then slowly pour the remaining oil in with the blades still running.

Once it's thickened again, add the rice vinegar and lemon juice, then blend for another 15 seconds. Let sit for 30 minutes to let flavors combine. Refrigerate until ready to use.

RECIPE FOUNDATIONS

FOOLPROOF WHITE RICE

Makes 3½ cups

CUISINE NOTE: It's so simple, yet surprisingly complex. When done right, Japanese style rice consists of fully separated, slightly sticky, delightfully chewy grains that have a soft sheen. One little mistake, though, and it can all go awry! A rice cooker helps with convenience, but cooking excellent rice on the stove is easy once you get the hang of it. Cooking rice is an art as much as it is a science, so be patient as you master the skill!

COOKING TIPS: Used too much heat, and now you have scorched rice on the bottom? No problem! That's called okoge, and many Japanese love the crunchy texture! Mix it into some rice balls, eat it as-is for a crunchy snack, or use it for okoge nabe (see recipe). Used too much water and now it's a little

mushy? Again, no problem. Mix it into some miso soup for a more filling meal.

Ingredients

- ☐ 1½ cups short grain Japanese rice
- ☐ 2 cups water (adjust as needed for your cooking equipment)
- ☐ 2 teaspoons salt

Instructions

First things first, wash the rice! Place the rice in a large bowl and add enough water to cover. Using your hands, softly scrub the grains together. The water will become cloudy as you polish the grains. Carefully pour out the cloudy water and add fresh water, repeating several times until the water is mostly clear. Transfer the rice to a colander and let drain completely.

Place the drained rice in a small pot with a tight fitting lid. Add the water and salt, then cover and turn the heat up to high. Stay with the pot, and once the water starts to boil, immediately turn the heat down to low. Simmer for 20 minutes, until all the water is absorbed.

Once the rice is cooked, turn off the burner, but leave the pot on the stove. Leave the lid on and let the rice rest for 10 minutes.

When ready to serve, use a spatula or rice ladle to gently fold the rice. Don't stir it, instead gently loosen the individual grains to create a fluffy texture.

SUSHI RICE

Makes 3½ cups

CUISINE NOTE: When we think of sushi, we think of raw fish, but the word comes from a Japanese word meaning sour rice, so it's really the rice that's at the heart of sushi. So if you're a little hesitant to make sushi at home, rest assured: you can have delicious sushi without raw fish, and it's still 100 percent authentic!

COOKING TIP: Sushi ingredients are served chilled, but the rice is actually room temperature. Cold rice becomes hard and chewy, so to make really good sushi, it's a delicate dance of temperatures and ingredients. But that doesn't mean it has to be hard! Just make the rice fresh and let it cool down on the counter before you use it.

Ingredients

- ☐ 3½ cups freshly cooked Japanese rice
- ☐ ¼ cup rice vinegar
- ☐ ¼ cup sugar
- ☐ 2 teaspoons salt

Instructions

In a small saucepan, combine the rice vinegar, sugar, and salt and heat until just warmed, not boiling. Stir until the sugar is dissolved, then remove from heat and let cool.

While still hot, transfer the freshly cooked rice to a large bowl.

Sprinkle the seasoned vinegar evenly over the top of the rice, then gently start folding the rice in on itself using a spatula. Take care not to squish the rice or apply pressure, the goal is to blend the vinegar over the rice, creating a subtle, sticky gloss over the individual grains.

Fan the rice while mixing to help it dry faster, and when it's cooled to room temperature, it's ready to use.

JAPANESE FISH STOCK (DASHI)

CUISINE NOTE: Dashi is an essential flavor to many Japanese dishes. It serves as the basis for the all-important fifth flavor: umami. Instant dashi granules are also a great choice, though you can use chicken or vegetable broth as a substitute.

COOKING TIP: Don't throw the used ingredients away! You can use them to make some homemade furikake, or rice seasoning. Use a knife to finely chop the ingredients, then place everything in a skillet over medium heat and stir until mostly dried. Add a tablespoon of soy sauce, a sprinkling of sesame, and you've got yourself an excellent rice topping. It doesn't last as long as the dried variety, but it's arguably even more delicious!

ICHIBAN DASHI

Makes 4 cups

Made with the freshest ingredients, this dashi is best suited for clear soups and dishes where dashi is a main flavor.

Ingredients

- ▢ 4 cups water
- ▢ 1 inch strip of kombu seaweed
- ▢ 1 ounce dried bonito flakes

Pour the water into a medium-sized pot and add the kombu.

Just before boiling, reduce heat to medium and let simmer for 15 minutes.

Remove the kombu, then bring the water to a boil.

Add the bonito flakes, then remove from heat.

Once the flakes have settled to the bottom, after about 2 minutes, remove any foam from the top, then filter the liquid through a cheesecloth-lined sieve.

Reserve the bonito and kelp for a second use.

NIBAN DASHI

Makes 4 cups

An economical way to get the most out of your ingredients, this second batch of dashi is best suited for miso soup and as a base in recipes building other flavors.

Ingredients

- 4 cups water
- Reserved bonito and kelp from ichiban dashi (above)
- ½ ounce dried bonito flakes

Take the reserved bonito and kelp and place in a medium sized pot with 4 cups of water.

Bring to a boil, then immediately turn heat down to medium and let simmer for 15 minutes.

Add the fresh bonito flakes, then remove from heat.

Once the flakes have settled to the bottom, after about 2 minutes, remove any foam from the top, then filter the liquid through a cheesecloth lined sieve.

VEGETARIAN DASHI

Makes 4 cups

A good dashi for vegetarians and meat eaters, the mushroom base adds an interesting complexity to dishes.

Ingredients

- 4 cups water
- 1 ounce dried shiitake mushrooms, about ¼ cup
- 1 inch strip of kombu seaweed

Place the water, mushrooms and kombu in a sealed container, then place in the fridge overnight. Strain the liquid before using.

JAPANESE FOOD CULTURE

Making Japanese food is one thing, but to really understand the food, an understanding of the culture is essential! While you may not be eating food in Japan, it's good to know proper Japanese food etiquette, so you can eat like a local, wherever in the world you may be. These are a few basic tips to know about Japanese food culture.

HOW TO USE CHOPSTICKS

While chopsticks are common in Japan, they aren't the only eating utensils used. Chopsticks are served with Japanese style meals, while a spoon and fork are served with Western style meals. As a foreigner, most Japanese will be impressed with even crude chopstick skills, so don't be afraid to struggle a bit! They appreciate the gesture!

1. Take one of the sticks and place in your dominant hand as if you would hold a pencil, but push the stick down until it's resting solidly between your thumb and first finger. The thumb serves as a stabilizer, so it shouldn't move much in your hand. Adjust it so only about an inch is sticking out past your thumb. Take your third finger and press it against the stick, so it's wedged solidly between your thumb and ring finger. The lower joint of the thumb will help to stabilize this stick, so these fingers should never move!

2. Take the second stick and place it against the tip of your thumb. Use your first and second fingers to press the stick in place. Using your first two fingers, you should be able to push the stick down using your first finger and up using your second finger.

3. To pick up food, start with the chopstick tips separated and position the sticks so that it's juuust a bit wider than the food you eat to grab. Slowly use your index finger to close the sticks together, then carefully pick it up and enjoy your food!

CHOPSTICK ETIQUETTE

1. Don't rest your chopsticks in your bowl. Either use a chopstick rest or place it on the paper liner of disposable chopsticks.

2. Don't stick your chopsticks in your food to rest either! It's reminiscent of an incense stick, which is common at funerals and honoring the dead, so doing so with your chopsticks is a bit of a bad omen. The same thing goes for passing food with chopsticks! Only pass with a plate, since doing so with chopsticks is similar to the ritual of passing cremated bones between chopsticks at funerals, so that's a big no-no!

3. You can pick up food with your chopsticks off a serving platter, just be sure to flip them around and use the fatter ends of the chopsticks so you're not spreading germs.

4. Don't wave your chopsticks around, point them at people, rub them together, stab food with them, or other types of general showiness, it comes off as a bit barbaric and rough. Just keep it chill.

5. Eat your soup with chopsticks! It may seem strange at first, but Japanese people typically eat the larger pieces of food with chopsticks, then hold the bowl to their mouth to drink the broth. Once you try it, you'll never want to use a spoon again!

TABLE ETIQUETTE

1. Seating arrangements matter! The middle of the table is the most important position, and those sitting on either side are the second most important. The host sits in the middle on the side closer to the door, while the honored guest sits in the middle on the other side.

2. To begin, restaurants generally hand you wet washcloths when you sit down. Don't use the towel on your face, just use it to wash your hands then fold it and put it aside.

3. Always begin any meal or snack by saying "Itadaki-masu" which means "I humbly receive." Then when you've finished the meal, say "Gochisosama-deshita," which roughly translates as "thank you for the feast."

4. Don't dump soy sauce directly on food, especially rice. Instead, just pour a small amount of soy sauce into a dipping bowl and dip your food into it. Don't pour too much, since you don't want to come off as wasteful.

5. Slurping is the highest praise! Slurping your noodles while eating is a sign that the food is just so good, you can't get enough! As well as being a compliment to the chef, it also cools down the noodles, making it easier to eat.

6. Do your best to clean up after yourself, meaning put everything back in its proper place. Place the lid back on your bowl, chopsticks on the rest, and in general just show respect to the food that just gave you nourishment.

7. A general rule of thumb is the person who invited everyone is the person who pays. Also, unless you're family or super close friends, people tend to order the same thing, going off of whatever the most important person at the table ordered. While it may seem strange, it's a sign of solidarity, everyone is in it together, which is very important to Japanese culture.

ANIME
GENRES

ADVENTURE & FANTASY

High calorie, energizing, and potentially portable food to boost your stamina over the long road ahead.

Easily the first thing that comes to mind when thinking of anime, adventure and fantasy are elements of most successful titles we see abroad, bringing us amazing titles such as Naruto, One Piece, Dragon Ball, Fairy Tail, and Pokémon, just to name a few. While they are distinct genres in their own right, it's hard to separate one genre from the other. For adventure, think of a young protagonist, off on an impossible journey to reach some ultimate goal, with lots of twists and turns along the way. For fantasy, think of supernatural abilities or whimsical components, whether it be magical powers or just superhuman ninja amazingness. Brought together, these genres weave together everything we love about storytelling: endearing heroes, larger than life villains, impossible odds, and an escape from our everyday reality. It's no wonder it's one of the biggest genres, it's just so entertaining!

Given the larger than life nature of many stories, the genre is typically embodied in many shonen titles, targeting younger men looking for energy and excitement in their entertainment. However, the depth of the stories are so well done that they are easily loved by fans of all ages.

A RECIPE FOR ADVENTURE

Start off with an endearingly mischievous main character. Not with ill intentions, just a bright eyed youth looking for excitement, perhaps a bit troublesome, but all in good fun. The back story is everything here, so we start slowly, bringing in a sprinkling of character development to tease out their natural sweetness.

Add in a pivotal movement, something that will change that character's life forever and set them down their true path. Of course, the unveiling of a long foretold prophecy is the cliché, but it could be something a little less fantastical: maybe crossing paths with the person who will soon become their lifelong rival, or perhaps a chance encounter with a mysterious mentor who guides them along their destined path. It could even be a sad experience, such as the death of a family member, destruction of their home, or crossing a line that the character can then never turn back on. We have to be careful with this though, for sadness has a very strong flavor and can quickly spoil the pot.

Next begins the delicate part, the transformation! Just as with a soufflé, timing and patience are everything: if pushed too fast too soon, the flavor will never fully develop, but go too slow and the dish will quickly fall flat. We give the character time to blossom, throwing in progressively bigger challenges as their skills develop. If done correctly, the energy of youthful vigor and hopefulness will soon permeate the kitchen. Once their flavor level is over 9000, you know you've got something delicious!

To really round out the flavor, choose a secret ingredient to draw you in. Maybe sprinkle in a little superhuman endurance, having them weather increasingly stronger blows that would break a mere mortal, or add a dash of magic, casting progressively fantastical spells. A personal favorite is a pinch of the supernatural, mixing in gods and spirits to make it feel a little more out of the ordinary. Perhaps you add in a little of all of this, but just remember: work the character delicately. Too much spice and you won't taste anything else!

Once peak form is achieved, it's time to put it to the test! A climactic moment to see how far they've come. A dramatic showdown, pitting hero against foe, good vs. evil, spicy vs. sweet...who will come out on top? Alas, you'll have to finish the dish to see!

BLACK BUTLER

Set in Victorian era England, the series follows Ciel Phantomhive, a thirteen-year-old boy who just so happens to be the head of his household, an aristocratic family known as the Queen's Guard Dog. Tasked with solving crimes in London's underworld, Ciel forms a contract with a demon, Sebastian, to seek revenge against his parents' murderer. Of course, you can't have a demon following you around everywhere without attracting attention, so Sebastian disguises himself as a loyal butler. In exchange for his unique services, he will be allowed to consume Ciel's soul when his revenge is complete. A little dark perhaps, but who doesn't love a good murder mystery?

While it may be set in England, they have quite the diverse selection of food! In one episode, the pair finds themselves in a curry competition—which is a wonderful competition to be in, is it not?! To win, they have to be unique, and Sebastian has just the thing up his sleeve: chocolate. Yes, you read that right. Innovative, yes, but innovative enough to win? Taste it yourself to see!

CHOCOLATE CURRY (CHOCO KARE)

Makes 8 servings

CUISINE NOTE: Curry might originate from India, but Japanese style curry has a unique taste all on its own. You can buy bricks of curry roux, which look a bit like a chocolate bar, but making it from scratch allows you to control the heat level to your liking.

COOKING TIP: While many curry recipes have you add the ingredients to the liquid, taking time to brown the meat and caramelize the onions helps develop a deeper flavor profile. While a bit more time consuming, it's worth it!

Ingredients

- [ ] 3 large onions, chopped
- [ ] 2 carrots, chopped
- [ ] 3 golden potatoes, chopped
- [ ] 1 small apple, grated
- [ ] 1 cup frozen peas
- [ ] 2 pounds beef stew meat, cut into bite size pieces
- [ ] 6 tablespoons butter, divided
- [ ] 3 tablespoons flour
- [ ] 3 tablespoons curry powder
- [ ] 1 tablespoon garam masala
- [ ] 2 cloves garlic, minced
- [ ] 3 tablespoons ketchup
- [ ] 8 cups beef stock
- [ ] Salt and pepper
- [ ] ½ bar chocolate, 1.55 oz
- [ ] ¼ cup cheddar cheese

Instructions

1. Place 2 tablespoons of butter and the chopped onions into a large pot over low heat. Cover with a tight fitting lid and cook for 40 minutes, stirring occasionally until the onions turn a deep caramel color.

2. Season the beef by sprinkling with salt and pepper. Add 1 tablespoon of butter to a wide skillet over medium high heat. When melted, add the beef and cook until browned. Remove from heat and set aside.

3. Once the onions are ready, add the beef, soup stock, grated apple, carrots, potatoes, garam masala, garlic, and ketchup to the pot containing the onions. Bring heat up to medium and simmer for 40 minutes.

4. Prepare the roux by placing the curry powder and remaining butter in a small pan over medium heat. Toast for a few minutes, until the spice smells fragrant and the mixture is bubbling. Add the flour, stirring for about a minute until a thick paste forms. Using a ladle, scoop a little bit of the liquid from the pot and add to the roux, stirring until blended. Continue slowly stirring liquid until it becomes a smooth gravy.

5. Add the roux, chocolate, and cheddar cheese to the pot and stir well. Continue simmering the pot for another 30 minutes. When ready to serve, add the peas, then cook for another 5 minutes. Serve with freshly cooked rice.

CURRY BREAD (ΚARE PAN)

Makes 12 servings

CUISINE NOTE: Japanese stuffed bread is the best thing since sliced bread! Light and fluffy, yet crunchy and delicious, it's a popular snack food, if you can manage to have some leftovers.

COOKING TIP: Don't have a kitchen thermometer? No problem! You can test it by dropping a piece of panko in the oil. If it starts to bubble and rise to the top immediately, it's ready.

Ingredients

- 2 teaspoons yeast
- 2 tablespoons sugar
- ½ cup lukewarm water
- 2 teaspoons salt
- 3½ cups flour, sifted
- 3 tablespoons unsalted butter, room temperature
- 2 tablespoons milk
- 1 cup water
- 3 cups leftover curry
- 2 eggs
- 2 cups panko bread crumbs

Instructions

1. Mix the yeast, sugar, and warm water in a large bowl and let sit for 10 minutes.

2. Add in the salt, flour, butter, and milk and mix to combine. Add just enough of the water until the dough forms into a ball, adding more water as needed.

3. Knead the dough on a lightly floured surface for about 10 minutes. Place the dough in a greased bowl, cover with plastic wrap or a towel, and let rise for about 60 minutes until doubled in size.

4. Punch down the dough, knead for 2 minutes, then place back into the bowl and let rise again for another hour.

5. While the dough is rising, prepare the curry by placing it in a small pot over medium heat. Let it simmer until it turns into a thick paste, mashing up larger chucks with a spoon. Remove from heat and let cool.

6. Punch down the dough, then divide into 12 pieces. To assemble a bun, flatten out the dough into a disk, thinning out the edges more than the middle. Place a spoonful of curry in the center, then gently fold up the sides to seal in the curry. Pinch the seams together, then place the bun seam side down on the counter to rest. Continue with the remaining dough.

7. Whisk the eggs in a small bowl, then place the panko on a small plate. Dip each bun in the eggs, then roll in the panko until evenly covered.

8. To fry, place some oil in a small pot over medium heat until it reaches around 375 degrees Fahrenheit. Place one or two buns in at a time without crowding the pot. Fry until golden brown, about 90 seconds per side, then transfer to paper towels to drain off excess oil.

9. Serve warm or at room temperature.

NARUTO

One of the most infamous anime titles abroad, the story follows the young ninja Naruto on his quest to become the most powerful ninja of all: Hokage, the village chief. Orphaned at a young age and struggling with the power of a tailed beast raging inside him, Naruto finds himself constantly alone, the villagers being understandably afraid of the monster within and keeping him at a distance. But that doesn't get him down! In fact, it's quite the opposite: he's determined to make friends and be strong enough to protect them, and when he sets his mind to something, nothing can stop him, for that is his ninja way!

Naruto faces many struggles, but nothing warms his heart quite like a bowl of ramen. Without a mother to cook for him, instant ramen is his go to meal, but when he gets treated to his favorite restaurant, Ichiraku, one bowl is never enough! Ramen is his chicken soup for the soul, and it's no wonder why. Savory, warm, nourishing, and filling, ramen is a classic Japanese comfort food meant to be slurped! If you're not eating it noisily, you're not doing it right!

ICHIRAKU RAMEN

Makes 6 servings

CUISINE NOTE: Ramen broth consists of two parts, the stock, typically made with bones to get more richness, and the tare, or seasonings. This version uses a soy sauce tare, but other popular flavors use miso or even salt to bring out the flavor.

COOKING TIP: Good ramen cannot be rushed! The broth takes a while, but it can be made ahead of time. Plus, the broth tastes even better the next day!

Ingredients

For Ramen

- [ ] 6 servings of ramen noodles, fresh or instant
- [ ] Soy marinated eggs (recipe below)
- [ ] Pickled bamboo shoots (recipe below)
- [ ] Green onion, chopped

For Soy Sauce Broth

- [ ] 12 cups water
- [ ] 2 pounds chicken bones
- [ ] 1 pound boneless pork shoulder or loin
- [ ] 3 cloves garlic, peeled
- [ ] 1 inch ginger, sliced
- [ ] 3 green onions, roughly chopped
- [ ] 1 cup soy sauce
- [ ] ¼ cup sake
- [ ] 2 tablespoons mirin

For Chashu Sauce

- [ ] ⅔ cup water
- [ ] ⅓ cup sake
- [ ] ⅓ cup soy sauce
- [ ] 3 tablespoons sugar

Instructions

1. Rinse the chicken bones under cold water, then place in a large stockpot with the water, pork, garlic, ginger and green onions. Bring to a boil, removing any grime that rises to the top. Turn the heat down and let simmer, covered, for about 2 hours.

2. Remove the pork, then strain the broth, discarding remaining ingredients. Add in 1 cup of soy sauce, ¼ cup sake, and 2 tablespoons mirin, then let simmer covered until ready to serve.

3. To finish the pork, combine the chashu sauce ingredients in a wide skillet. Add the pork, then bring to a simmer over medium heat. Place a lid on top, left slightly ajar for steam to escape, then turn heat down to low and simmer for about 30 minutes, turning the meat occasionally, until there is only a little liquid left. Remove the lid, remaining with the skillet, watching the liquid simmer until bubbles start to appear. Turn the pork over to fully coat it in the sauce, then remove from the pan and slice thinly.

4. When ready to serve, cook the ramen according to package directions. Divide the broth among 6 bowls, then add in the noodles, topping with pork, pickles bamboo shoots, soy marinated eggs, and green onions. Serve piping hot!

RAMEN TOPPING: BAMBOO SHOOTS (MENMA)

Ingredients

- 1 can (8 oz) bamboo shoots, cut into strips
- 1 cup dashi stock
- 1 tablespoon soy sauce
- 1 tablespoon sake
- 2 teaspoons sugar
- 1 teaspoon salt

Combine all ingredients in a small pot and bring to a simmer over medium heat. Continue simmering for about 20 minutes until most of the liquid has absorbed. Remove from heat and let cool.

RAMEN TOPPING: SOY MARINATED EGGS

Ingredients

- 6 large eggs
- 3 tablespoons soy sauce
- 3 tablespoons mirin
- 3 tablespoons water

Bring a small pot filled with water to a boil. Add eggs, then immediately cover and reduce heat to medium low. Simmer for 7 minutes, then drain and immediately place eggs in a bowl of ice water.

Gently peel the eggs, then place in a Ziploc bag. Add the soy sauce, mirin and water and close, removing as much air from the bag as possible. Place the bag in the fridge to marinate for at least 4 hours, up to a day.

NOT SO INSTANT INSTANT RAMEN

Makes 6 servings

CUISINE NOTE: Cheap packaged instant ramen is loved just as much in Japan as it is by college students abroad. But just because it's cheap doesn't mean it has to stay cheap. Add some added nutrition by mixing in leftovers or frozen items in your fridge.

COOKING TIP: Want to be really authentic? Cook your egg in the soup! Crack an egg into the ramen as it's simmering on the stove, and let it cook for about 4 minutes until it just starts to set.

Ingredients

- 1 package instant ramen
- 1 tablespoon sesame oil
- ¼ cup cooked protein (pulled pork, chicken, tofu, etc.)
- ¼ cup mixed vegetables (frozen corn or peas, sliced bell pepper, onions)
- 1 egg, hard boiled or just cooked
- 2 teaspoons sesame seeds

Cook the ramen according to package directions.

While the ramen is cooking, prepare your toppings. Add the sesame oil to a wide skillet over medium heat. When hot, add the protein and cook for 2–3 minutes until the edges start to sear. Move to the side of the pan and add in the vegetables. Cook for another 2–3 minutes until just softened, then remove from heat and set aside.

Once the ramen is done, transfer to a serving bowl and add the toppings on top. Sprinkle with sesame seeds and additional drizzle of sesame oil, if desired.

WORLD TRIGGER

A gate to another universe suddenly opens in Osamu Mikumo's hometown, and strange beings called Neighbors start pouring in. Looking to gather trion, a magical power residing untapped within us, these Neighbors start an invasion, attacking the city and kidnapping citizens. The Border Defense Agency is soon created, quickly managing to secure the city and build a massive base as their headquarters. Wanting to help, Osamu enlists in the attempt to protect their home. What is the nature of this foreign race and the world beyond the portal? What really is trion, and why do they want it? Osamu is determined to find out!

While the story follows Osamu, the real entertainment comes in his interactions with more colorful characters, my favorite being Jin Yuichi. While Jin's laid back personality and incessant munching on rice crackers make him appear to be a slacker, he's actually a high ranking member within Border. He serves as a good reminder that no matter how serious things get, it's important to keep a positive mindset, and having some snacks always helps! Instead of frying, I prefer to bake my crackers instead. A little less oil, though just as satisfying!

RICE CRACKERS (SENBEI)

Makes 32 crackers

CUISINE NOTE: Senbei are popular as souvenirs, with local variations being proudly displayed in pretty packaging. Whether they are made at home or acquired from afar, senbei are delicious!

COOKING TIP: Thinness is everything here! Too fat and it will feel like eating a brick, and potentially retain too much moisture, turning them stale. Go easy on the oil, and try to get even thickness throughout the crackers for consistent baking.

Ingredients

- [ ] 2 teaspoons soy sauce, divided
- [ ] 2 teaspoons mirin
- [ ] ¾ cup rice flour
- [ ] ½ cup cooked white rice
- [ ] ¼ cup water
- [ ] 2 tablespoons furikake, plus additional for sprinkling
- [ ] Vegetable oil

Instructions

1. Preheat oven to 375 degrees F. Combine 1 teaspoon soy sauce and mirin in a small bowl and set aside.

2. To make the dough, place the rice flour, cooked rice, furikake, and one teaspoon of soy sauce in a food processor. Run until the mixture clumps into a ball, adding water as needed. Remove from the processor and roll into a ball.

3. Divide the dough into 4 equal portions, then roll out the portions into logs. Cut each log into 8 disks.

4. To shape the crackers, place dough on a greased baking sheet, and using a glass with a flat bottom, press the balls into a circle. The dough will be sticky, so use oil liberally to prevent sticking. If needed, flatten the dough out further with your hands, getting the crackers as thin as possible without breaking them.

5. Place the baking sheet in the middle rack and bake for 8 minutes. Flip the crackers over and bake for 8–10 more minutes, until the tops start to brown.

6. Remove the crackers from the oven and immediately brush with the mirin mixture. Lightly sprinkle additional furikake on top. Bake for another 3 minutes until the glaze is browned, then remove from the oven. Let cool completely on a wire rack before serving.

BUNGO STRAY DOGS

A starving orphan alone on the streets, Nakajima Atsushi suddenly finds himself in the company of some strange men. They are members of the Armed Detective Agency who work to solve incidents other agencies won't touch. With a man-eating tiger on the loose, they're out to catch it, and Atsushi suddenly finds himself coming along for the ride. Can they find it before it kills again? With some mystical powers and solid detective work, it's just another day for the Agency.

Dealing with supernatural powers, the team has had their fair share of unique characters. Atsushi finds a kindred spirit in Kyouka Izumi, who was manipulated into being an assassin at a young age. Empathizing with the emotional abuse she endured over the years, he can't help but want to help her. Wanting to give her a taste of normal life, he ends up taking her on a date around Yokohama. And what do they do? Eat crepes!

JAPANESE STYLE STREET CREPES

Makes 10 crepes

CUISINE NOTE: Head to any touristy crowded area in Tokyo, and chances are you are going to come across a crepe store. With tempting windows displaying rows of colorful sweet crepes, it's hard to resist! They use very wide crepe pans, making large crepes wrapped in paper for a portable snack to enjoy while strolling around.

COOKING TIP: The batter should be thin to ensure it can quickly be swirled to cover the pan while cooking. If it seems a little too thick, add a little bit of water to make it more runny.

Ingredients

- [ ] 2 cups white flour, sifted
- [ ] 3 eggs, beaten
- [ ] 1 ½ cups milk
- [ ] 1 tablespoon unsalted butter, melted
- [ ] 1 tablespoon sugar
- [ ] 1 teaspoon vanilla extract
- [ ] ¼ teaspoon salt
- [ ] Vegetable oil
- [ ] For fillings: whipped cream, Nutella, fruit, ice cream, syrup, etc.

Instructions

1. Sift the flour, sugar, and salt into a large bowl. Gradually add the eggs, butter, and milk, mixing until the batter is perfectly smooth. Let batter stand at room temperature for 30 minutes.

2. When ready to cook, heat a tablespoon of oil in a wide non-stick frying pan over medium heat. Add about ⅓ cup of batter to the pan and swirl to spread the batter all over the pan. Cook for 2 minutes until the bottom is golden brown, then carefully flip the crepe and cook 1 minute before removing from pan. Repeat with the remaining batter.

3. To assemble, place a crepe on the counter. Pipe whipped cream or other filling evenly across a quarter circle of the surface. Place fruit or ice cream on top as desired, then drizzle with syrup or matcha powder. To fold, first fold in half so the filling is on one side, then fold the unfilled side on top. Place on a plate and drizzle with additional syrup before serving.

BLACK CLOVER

In a world where magic is everything, it may come as a surprise to see churches still have their place in society, but luckily for young Asta and Yuno, the church was there to take them in! Abandoned as babies, Yuno has grown up gifted with exceptional magical powers, while Asta is the only one in this world without any at all! But that doesn't stop Asta from dreaming! The pair both receive grimoires on their fifteenth birthday, but Asta's is anything but normal. A rare book that negates and repels his opponent's spells, he may just be able to make something of himself after all! Can one of them manage to reach the ultimate goal, being the Wizard King?!

Growing up in a church, the brothers learn at an early age the value of money and charity. Living mainly off what they can grow themselves, potatoes are the bread and butter of their daily life. Potato this, potato that...it must be hard not to grow tired of them! On their last meal before they set off on their journey to become the Wizard King, everyone cooks them a magnificent feast...of potatoes of course! One of my favorite ways to enjoy potatoes is in tempura, it's like Japanese style fries. Of course, you can mix other vegetables in too—everything tastes better when it's deep fried!

SWEET POTATO TEMPURA

Makes 4 servings

CUISINE NOTE: With tempura ingredients, really anything goes. Root vegetables, leafy vegetables, mushrooms, shrimp—it's like in America: everything tastes better when it's deep fried, even ice cream! Though that one is a bit trickier to pull off.

COOKING TIP: Chilled batter is essential for light and crispy texture. Don't over-stir either, otherwise you risk activating the gluten in the flour.

Ingredients

- 2 sweet potatoes
- 1 large egg
- ¾ cup water
- 1 cup all-purpose flour, sifted
- ¾ cup dashi
- 3 tablespoons soy sauce
- 3 tablespoons mirin
- 1 tablespoon sugar

Instructions

1. Prepare the sauce by combining the dashi, mirin, sugar, and soy sauce in a small saucepan. Bring to a boil, then lower the heat and let it simmer until sugar is dissolved. Remove from heat and let cool.

2. Prepare the sweet potato by thinly slicing into rounds, then soaking in water for 15 minutes to remove excess starch. Pat dry with paper towels.

3. Place the egg and water in a small bowl and whisk to combine. Skim off any foam from the surface, then slowly pour the egg into the flour. Be careful not to over stir, and leave a few lumps in the batter for texture.

4. Place just enough oil to cover the potato slices in a small pot. Bring the oil to a temperature of 325 degrees F. Working with a few slices at a time, quickly dip the slices in the batter and place in the oil. Fry for 2 minutes, then remove from oil and let drain on paper towels.

5. Serve immediately with dipping sauce on the side.

ONE PIECE

Forget Blackbeard, the ultimate pirate of legend is the world renowned Pirate King, Gol D. Roger. When he was finally captured, he revealed that his treasure, the One Piece, was hidden somewhere along the treacherous Grand Line. Fast forward twenty-two years after his death, a young boy Monkey D. Luffy sets off to find it himself, gathering a ragtag crew of misfits along the way. After eating the Gum-Gum Fruit, he is now a man made of rubber, which definitely helps him get out of some tough situations. Is he destined to become the next Pirate King? With the support of his friends, he just might!

The favorite character of many, the adorable reindeer Chopper ate the Human-Human Fruit and can now speak! What does he do with this ability? Become a doctor of course, to help the humans who helped him. And if that wasn't enough of a super power, he puts his medical knowledge to use to create Rumble Balls which activate different abilities within him. But have fans of the show ever wondered what's really in them? Pop one of those things in your mouth and suddenly all sorts of amazing powers can be unleashed, it's magic! A part of me has always thought, there's got to be some type of alcohol in there. What I sometimes like to call liquid courage, a shot or two of rum can get me just loose enough to unleash some of my own inner power. Just a little bit goes a long way, so do eat responsibly!

RUM-BLE BALLS

Makes 20 balls

CUISINE NOTE: While famous for sake, Japan also has quite a selection of whisky and rum!

COOKING TIP: As you mix everything together, it might seem a little runny at first. Don't panic! It will firm up as it sits in the fridge, but you can always add in a little more crumbled biscuits to firm it up. Serve chilled, and the texture is exquisite, almost like fudge!

Ingredients

- ☐ 1 batch Sesame Shortbread Cookies (see recipe)
- ☐ 2 cups pecans
- ☐ ⅓ cup honey
- ☐ 1 teaspoon vanilla extract
- ☐ ½ cup rum
- ☐ Sugar for dusting

Instructions

1. Place the shortbread in a food processor and process until finely ground. Transfer to a large bowl.

2. Add pecans in the processor and process until roughly chopped. Add to the crumbled shortbread, along with the honey and rum.

3. Use a spoon to portion out into 1 inch balls, rolling with your hands to smooth. Roll the balls in sugar to dust the surface, then place in an airtight container and place in refrigerator until ready to serve.

SESAME SHORTBREAD COOKIES

Makes 3 dozen cookies

Ingredients

- ☐ 1 cup butter, softened
- ☐ 1 ¾ cups all-purpose flour, sifted
- ☐ ¼ cup rice flour
- ☐ ½ cup powdered sugar
- ☐ ½ cup granulated sugar
- ☐ 1 teaspoon vanilla extract
- ☐ ½ teaspoon salt
- ☐ 1 teaspoon sesame seeds

Instructions

1. Preheat the oven to 325 degrees Fahrenheit.

2. Combine the butter, vanilla, powdered sugar and granulated sugar in a large bowl. Stir until well blended.

3. In a separate bowl, sift the flour and salt together, then stir into the wet ingredients. Mix until the dough combines into a smooth ball.

4. Roll the dough out to ¼ inch thickness on a lightly floured surface. Cut into desired shapes, then place 2 inches apart on a greased cookie sheet. Sprinkle with sesame seeds, gently pressing the seeds into the surface with your hands.

5. Bake in the oven for 9–11 minutes, until the tops are just barely golden brown. Transfer to a wire rack to cool.

HUNTER X HUNTER

Gon Freecss was told all his life that both his parents were dead. When he learns that his father is still alive after all, and an accomplished Hunter at that, he sets off to follow in his footsteps. Hunters are the epitome of cool, risking their lives to seek hidden treasures, exotic creatures, headhunting, and all sorts of adventures. Can Gon become "the Best Hunter in the World" and meet his father? It won't be easy, but with the right attitude, and support of his friends, there's no hurdle too big.

For aspiring Hunters, finding the test is a test in itself. After many trials, Gon finds himself at the test site, but there's no test in sight! Only a restaurant, and a tonkatsu restaurant at that. But things are not always as they appear. Speak the right word, and you'll earn yourself passage to the back room. Of course, Gon makes it through and finds the true entrance to the hunter exam, but it's a shame he didn't sit down and eat before he went. Freshly cooked tonkatsu is almost too hard to pass up!

FRIED PORK CUTLETS (TONKATSU)

Makes 4 servings

CUISINE NOTE: Tonkatsu falls under the category of *yoshoku*, which consists of Western-Japanese fusion cooking. These days tonkatsu is pork, but originally, the dish was typically made with beef. Delicious as is, it's also served in a sandwich, or simmered with onions over a bed of rice.

COOKING TIP: You can serve the cabbage as is, but submerging it in saltwater for a few minutes gives it a little extra depth and flavor.

Ingredients

- 4 slices pork loin
- Salt and pepper, to taste
- ½ cup flour, for dredging
- 2 cups panko
- 2 eggs, lightly beaten
- ½ head napa cabbage, shredded
- ½ cup tonkatsu sauce

Instructions

1. Thinly slice the cabbage, then place the shredded in a bowl of cold water mixed with a teaspoon of salt. Let sit for 15 minutes.

2. Pat dry the pork loin with paper towels, then sprinkle with salt and pepper.

3. Dredge each pork chop in flour, then dip into the beaten eggs and press into the bread crumbs, coating both sides.

4. Heat about a ½ inch of oil in a small pot over medium heat. When the temperature reaches 350 degrees, add one cutlet to the pan and fry for 5–7 minutes, flipping it over halfway, until it turns golden brown. Remove from the pot and transfer to paper towels to drain. Repeat the process with the remaining slices.

5. To serve, drain the cabbage thoroughly and arrange on plates. Cut each cutlet into thin strips, then place alongside the cabbage. Serve with tonkatsu sauce.

PORK CUTLETS OVER RICE (KATSUDON)

Makes 4 servings

CUISINE NOTE: If you see *"don"* at the end of a dish, it means it's a bowl of rice with some sort of topping. Typically this implies a topping with some sort of sauce, allowing it to soak down into the rice and give it extra flavor. Some restaurants make a point of brushing an additional coat of sauce over the rice before adding the topping, to ensure the rice is extra delicious!

COOKING TIP: Leftover fried food loses its crunchiness, but this dish actually works great with the softened breading. But, if you really want that crunch, you can place the leftover pork in the oven at 350 degrees Fahrenheit for about 10 minutes to help bring some of the crispiness back.

Ingredients:

- 1 tablespoon sesame oil
- ¼ onion, sliced
- ¼ cup shredded cabbage
- ¼ cup dashi
- 1 cup cooked rice
- ½ tablespoon mirin
- ½ tablespoon sugar
- 1 tablespoon soy sauce
- 1 egg

- 1 serving tonkatsu, sliced
- 1 green onion, chopped

Instructions

1. Place a frying pan over medium heat and add the oil. When hot, add the onion and cabbage and cook for 5 minutes, until the onion has softened.

2. Combine the dashi, mirin, soy sauce and sugar and add to the pan. Stir to coat the onions and cabbage, then place the tonkatsu slices on top. Cover the pan with a loose fitting lid and let simmer for 5 minutes.

3. Gently beat the egg, then pour around the sides of the tonkatsu. Sprinkle green onions on top, then cover with the lid and cook until the egg is just set. Remove from heat, then pour the contents of the skillet over a bowl of freshly cooked rice. Sprinkle with additional green onion to serve.

BLUE EXORCIST

Being orphaned at an early age, twins Rin and Yukio Okumura have been raised by Father Fujimoto, a kind hearted priest and famous exorcist. Not really buying into the whole demon thing, Rin tries his best to be a good kid, but he can't live up to his brother in terms of school, and try as he might, he always seems to be getting into trouble. Just when he finally seems to be getting on the right path, he discovers a secret about his past.... He's actually the son of Satan! Not wanting to be defined by his family tree, he sets off to become an exorcist alongside his brother, aiming to one day defeat Satan himself!

One endearing thing about Rin is his good heart. While he gets into trouble, he really does have good intentions. His failure of a first job is a prime example: how much trouble can you really get into at a grocery store? A lot, apparently! While his mishaps eventually push the store manager to her breaking point, he does manage to get customers excited by serving them samples of some really good yakisoba! He knows the best way to sell food is to get people to taste it, and what better recipe to make than quick, delicious, satisfying noodles!

YAKISOBA

Makes 4 servings

CUISINE NOTE: This quick stir fried dish can be served with soba noodles as done below, but it's also excellent with udon. Soba offers thin, almost nutty flavored noodles, while udon give a nice chewy, thick bite. Try both and see which you prefer!

COOKING TIP: A really good pan with a nonstick surface is essential for this dish. It cooks quickly, and you can mix in all sorts of veggies and meats. A good dish for a beginning cook to get creative!

Ingredients

- [ ] 1 tablespoon sugar
- [ ] 1 tablespoon soy sauce
- [ ] 1 tablespoon oyster sauce
- [ ] 2 tablespoons ketchup
- [ ] 2 tablespoons Worcestershire sauce
- [ ] 1 onion
- [ ] 1 carrot
- [ ] 3 shiitake mushrooms
- [ ] 3 green onions
- [ ] ¼ head of cabbage
- [ ] 1 pound pork chops
- [ ] 2 tablespoons sesame oil
- [ ] 4 servings soba noodles

Instructions

1. Whisk the sugar, soy sauce, oyster sauce, ketchup, and Worcestershire sauce in a small bowl and set aside.

2. Cook the noodles according to the package directions, then set aside in a bowl.

3. Prepare the vegetables by slicing the onion, carrot, cabbage, and mushrooms into thin strips. Chop the green onion into 2 inch pieces, then finally cut meat into bite sized pieces.

4. Add the oil to a wide skillet or wok and place over medium heat. Add the pork, then cook until it's no longer pink.

5. Add the onion and carrot and cook for another 2 minutes, then add the cabbage and cook until almost tender. Lastly, add the green onion and mushrooms and cook for 1 minute.

6. Separate the soba gently with your hands, then add the noodles to the skillet and lower heat to medium. Pour the sauce over the skillet, using tongs to mix everything together. When most of the liquid has been absorbed, transfer to bowls and serve immediately.

COMEDY

Dishes to satiate your cravings and provide a healthy dose of soul food to lift your spirits and brighten your day.

Many people use anime as a form of escape, and what better way to escape your stressful everyday life with some lighthearted fun? In some sense, Westerners view Japan as a steadfast, serious country: hardworking salarymen diligently working eighty hours a week, studious children attending nightly cram schools to increase their chances of academic success, even mothers working endlessly to provide the best support for her family. But all that seriousness means they really need some good stress release, so naturally they turn to some good entertainment. This may be why anime tends to do comedy really well.

While most series have some elements of humor in them, some bring comedy to the forefront, making it an essential element of the story. When thinking of a comedy series, they typically feature elements of normal everyday life, but use that as the perfect contrasting setting for some genuinely silly, entertaining situations. Given that everyone needs a good laugh, the titles span all genres and age groups. In fact, some of the best ones loved by all ages are actually aimed at a younger age group, which just goes to show, good clean humor is good for everyone!

A DISH TO RAISE THE LOWEST OF SPIRITS

A good comedy should taste like home. Nothing too crazy or far reaching, just elements of every day with a touch of flair. Start off by picking a relatable story: a well-meaning youth, a striving young office worker, perhaps an endearing character with a quirky hobby. Start off slow, building a solid base flavor by carefully by setting the stage. What makes this person tick, how can we relate to them? Pick one or two strong spices to permeate the dish. Perhaps a base of unwavering optimism, a dash of youthful inspiration, maybe toss in a stoic demeanor that allows them to work through the toughest of situations. Take time at the beginning to build the character to ensure proper texture.

Once the main character has been set, it's time to spice things up! Mix in a few surprising ingredients: colorful mishaps, failed experiments, perhaps a few silly misunderstandings. Nothing too serious or heavy, you don't want to flavor to fall flat, add just enough drama to build comedic effect. Include a pinch of backstory, just enough sadness to make them more relatable, for after all, a good protagonist shouldn't be too perfect, it should taste familiar, but not boring.

After a few carefully timed catastrophes, bring it all together to end on a high flavor note. Our protagonist should always come out swinging, giving us hope and energy to sustain us through our everyday battles. A sweet taste that lingers does wonders for creating warmth in the heart.

THE DISASTROUS LIFE OF SAIKI K.

If the show's name isn't enough to give it away, Kusuo Saiki is not your normal high school student. Born with all manner of psychic abilities, he can use them to get whatever he wants, but he knows that using his powers always comes at a cost. It's tempting to think it might go to Kusuo's head, but actually it's quite the opposite, he tries his hardest just to blend in. Of course, the harder he tries, the more disastrous it gets! He's kept his powers in check so far, but with the temptations of high school now on his mind, will he be able to resist bending all the rules—and spoons?

His life might be a little hectic at times, but Kusuo knows how to enjoy the little things when they come. His indulgence of choice: coffee jelly. Give him a bowl of jelly, and everything seems to turn out ok in the end. Get in the way of his jelly, and there's no telling what will happen!

COFFEE JELLY

Makes 4 servings

CUISINE NOTE: Japanese desserts make jellies with agar, a seaweed, but gelatin gives a much better texture to pair with whipped cream.

COOKING TIP: As a former barista, I recommend adding a pinch of cinnamon to your coffee before brewing! It adds a little hint of flavor to your cup, but doesn't overwhelm the coffee. And to reduce bitterness, throw in a pinch of salt too!

Ingredients

- ☐ 2 cups hot coffee
- ☐ 1 tablespoon unflavored gelatin
- ☐ 2 tablespoons sugar
- ☐ Dash of cinnamon

Instructions

1. Mix together the gelatin and sugar. Pour freshly brewed hot coffee into a mixing bowl and whisk in the powdered ingredients. Stir until dissolved.

2. Pour liquid into 4 individual cups, or pour into a square baking dish and place in the refrigerator to set. Let chill for about 4 hours until completely firm.

3. If it was chilled in a square dish, use a sharp knife to cut into 1 inch cubes and gently scoop out into individual bowls. Top with whipped cream and cinnamon to serve.

MATCHA JELLY

Makes 4 servings

Ingredients

- ☐ ½ cup milk
- ☐ 1 ½ cups boiling water
- ☐ 1 tablespoon unflavored gelatin
- ☐ 2 tablespoons sugar
- ☐ 1 tablespoon matcha powder

Instructions

1. Mix together the matcha powder, gelatin, and sugar. Pour boiling water into mixing bowl and whisk in the powdered ingredients. Stir until dissolved.

2. Let the liquid cool for a minute or so, then stir in the milk. Pour liquid into 4 individual cups, or pour into a square baking dish and place in the refrigerator to set. Let chill for about 4 hours until completely firm.

3. If chilled in a square dish, use a sharp knife to cut into 1 inch cubes and gently scoop out into individual bowls. Top with whipped cream and dust with extra matcha powder to serve.

HAIKYUU!!

With a passion for volleyball but no team to play with, middle schooler Hinata Shouyou is determined to play one way or another. After finally gathering enough players in his final year, he gets to compete in an actual competition—only to face off against star player Kageyama Tobio in the very first round. Though they suffer a crushing defeat, Hinata vows to become better and surpass Kageyama. Starting high school, he joins a team determined to wipe the floor with Kageyama the next time they meet on the court...or at least that was the plan. Upon discovering that Kageyama is on the same team, they have to learn to work together if either of them want to play. Sounds like the perfect recipe for trouble, doesn't it?

As you can imagine, being forced to play with your sworn enemy is no easy task. The path ahead of them is far from smooth, but food works wonders to bring people together. After a pivotal team building moment, the team grabs some steamed buns from the local convenience store to strengthen their newfound bonds. A great way to celebrate, as long as they learn how to share!

STEAMED BUNS (NIKUMAN)

Makes 20 small buns

CUISINE NOTE: The Japanese version of Chinese *baozi*, these white and fluffy steamed buns are traditionally filled with pork. The key to a really good bun is to ensure that the meat isn't too dense. As you tear the bun, the filling should tear too.

COOKING TIP: Don't have a steamer? You can use a microwave! The texture is denser, but hey, it still works! Place a bun on microwave safe plate, dampen with a teaspoon of water, then cover with plastic wrap. Turn the power level down to 70 percent, then for a small bun, microwave for 60 seconds. Be careful not to overcook! Larger buns cook for around 2 minutes.

Ingredients

For the Dough

- ☐ 2 ½ cups all-purpose flour
- ☐ 2 tablespoons granulated sugar
- ☐ ½ teaspoon salt
- ☐ 1 ½ teaspoons baking powder
- ☐ 1 teaspoon instant dry yeast
- ☐ 1 tablespoons vegetable oil
- ☐ ¾ cup water

For the Filling

- ☐ ¾ pound ground pork
- ☐ 2 green onions, chopped
- ☐ 1 can water chestnuts, chopped
- ☐ 1 teaspoon salt
- ☐ 1 inch ginger, grated
- ☐ 1 teaspoon granulated sugar
- ☐ 1 tablespoon sake
- ☐ 1 tablespoon soy sauce
- ☐ 1 tablespoon sesame oil
- ☐ 1 tablespoon cornstarch

Instructions

1. First, prepare the dough. Combine the flour, sugar, salt, baking powder, yeast and oil in a large bowl. Slowly add the water, stirring to combine. Mix until fully incorporated.

2. Place the dough on a lightly floured surface and knead for about 10 minutes, until the dough becomes smooth and elastic. Sprinkle with additional flour as needed to reduce stickiness, but resist the urge to add too much as it will become less sticky as its worked.

3. Roll the dough into a ball, place in a greased bowl, and cover in plastic wrap or a towel. Sit in a warm place to rise until doubled in size, about an hour.

4. While the dough is rising, prepare the filling. In a large bowl, combine all of the filling ingredients and mix well. Place in the fridge until ready to use.

5. Once the dough has doubled in size, dust the working surface with flour and divide the dough evenly into 20 pieces. Prepare some parchment paper by cutting it out into 3 inch squares.

6. Working with one piece of dough at a time, flatten it out into a disk, and place a spoonful of filling in the middle. Very gently start pulling at the dough and bringing it up over the top of the filling. As you pull up each section, pinch it together to seal the dough. Once all the edges have been pulled up, pinch the middle together and place seam side down on a parchment paper square. Repeat with the remaining dough, then let the buns rest for 15 minutes.

7. Add an inch of water to a wide skillet or wok. Once the water

is boiling, place the buns on parchment paper in the steamer tray, leaving about an inch between each bun. Close the lid and steam over high heat for 12 minutes. Serve hot.

NASHVILLE HOT CHICKEN STEAMED BUNS

Makes 20 small buns

CUISINE NOTE: While ground pork is the classic filling, you can put just about anything inside! To give you an idea of some possibilities, this fun twist brings a fusion cuisine of two of my favorite dishes.

COOKING TIP: Cooking the chicken beforehand makes steaming a little easier, and helps the filling stay tighter within the dough. A little extra work up front, but the end result is worth it!

Ingredients

For the Dough
- ☐ 2 ½ cups all-purpose flour
- ☐ 2 tablespoons granulated sugar
- ☐ ½ teaspoon salt
- ☐ 1 ½ teaspoons baking powder
- ☐ 1 teaspoon instant dry yeast
- ☐ 1 tablespoons vegetable oil
- ☐ ¾ cup water

For the Filling
- ☐ ¾ pound chicken thighs, deboned, skinned and chopped into small pieces
- ☐ 1 cup dill pickle juice
- ☐ 1 jalapeno pepper, diced
- ☐ 2 tablespoons Louisiana-style hot sauce
- ☐ ¼ cup salt
- ☐ 1 cup water
- ☐ 3 tablespoons cornstarch
- ☐ 2 teaspoons smoked paprika
- ☐ 2 teaspoons ground cayenne pepper
- ☐ 1 teaspoon kosher salt
- ☐ ½ teaspoon finely ground black pepper
- ☐ ¼ cup chopped dill pickle
- ☐ 2 tablespoons mayonnaise
- ☐ Oil for frying

For the Dipping Sauce
- ☐ 1 tablespoon cayenne pepper
- ☐ 1 teaspoon smoked paprika
- ☐ 1 teaspoon ground cumin
- ☐ 2 tablespoons Louisiana-style hot sauce
- ☐ ½ teaspoon garlic powder
- ☐ ½ tablespoon salt
- ☐ 1 teaspoon sugar
- ☐ ½ cup vegetable oil

Instructions

1. Prepare a brine by combining the dill pickle juice, diced jalapeno, hot sauce, salt, and water in a

large bowl. Place the chicken in the brine, arranging it so it is fully covered. Place in the fridge to marinate for 4–8 hours.

2. Prepare the dipping sauce by combining all ingredients in a small bowl. Set aside to let the flavors fully combine.

3. When ready to cook, first prepare the dough by combining the flour, sugar, salt, baking powder, yeast and oil in a large bowl. Slowly add the water, stirring to combine. Mix until fully incorporated.

4. Place the dough on a lightly floured surface and knead for about 10 minutes, until the dough becomes smooth and elastic. Sprinkle with additional flour as needed to reduce stickiness, but resist the urge to add too much as it will become less sticky as its worked.

5. Roll the dough into a ball, place in a greased bowl, and cover in plastic wrap or a towel. Sit in a warm place to rise until doubled in size, about an hour.

6. While the dough is rising, prepare the chicken. Remove the chicken from the brine and pat dry with paper towels. Combine the cornstarch, smoked paprika, cayenne pepper, salt and pepper in

a small bowl, then add the chicken. Toss to coat.

7. Add enough oil to cover the chicken in a small pot and place over medium high heat. When hot, add a couple of spoonfuls of chicken at a time to the pot, fry for 4–5 minutes until the chicken is golden brown. Remove from the oil with a slotted spoon, then place on paper towels to drain. Repeat with remaining chicken.

8. Prepare the filling by mixing the fried chicken, pickles, and mayonnaise in a small bowl.

9. Once the dough has doubled in size, dust the working surface with flour and divide the dough evenly into 20 pieces. Prepare some parchment paper by cutting it out into 3 inch squares.

10. Working with one piece of dough at a time, flatten it out into a disk, and place a spoonful of filling in the middle. Very gently start pulling at the dough and bringing it up over the top of the filling. As you pull up each piece, pinch it together to seal the dough. Once all the edges have been pulled up, pinch the middle together and place seam side down on a parchment paper square. Repeat with the remaining dough, then let the buns rest for 15 minutes.

11. Add an inch of water to a wide skillet or wok. Once the water is boiling, place the buns on parchment paper in the steamer tray, leaving about an inch between each bun. Close the lid and steam over high heat for 8 minutes. Serve hot with dipping sauce on the side.

ONE PUNCH MAN

Some people are superheroes for fame and glory, others because they feel like it's the right thing to do. In Saitama's case, he does it just for fun. But when training and pushing yourself to your limit is your source of fun, what do you do when you're just too strong? It's been far too long since Saitama had a good fight, now being able to finish off any opponent in just one punch. Can he finally find an opponent to give his life some meaning, or is he doomed to a life of boredom?

A superhero story that also pokes fun at superhero stories, One Punch Man is a lighthearted take on the genre that makes the genre even better. For example, Saitama's first villain encounter. Ever find yourself eating so much crab that you just become a crab in the process? Happens to the best of us; you are what you eat, after all. The villain found himself in just that situation, becoming a crab powered monster after evening of crab feasting! Let's indulge in some delectable crab dishes ourselves, but remember, all things in moderation! Unless a crab power is what you're going for. If so, by all means, indulge!

SIMMERED CRAB RICE
(KANI MESHI)

Makes 4 servings

CUISINE NOTE: Cooking rice with broth and other ingredients is a dish called *takikomi gohan*. This allows the flavor to fully penetrate the rice grains, blending the flavors beautifully.

COOKING TIP: Keep the temperature low, otherwise the bottom of the rice might burn! If it happens, that's ok. Called *okoge*, people sometimes intentionally burn the pot to get a crispy rice bottom.

Ingredients

- [ ] 2 cups crab meat, shredded
- [ ] 2 cup of rice
- [ ] 2 cups dashi
- [ ] 1 tablespoon soy sauce
- [ ] 2 tablespoons mirin
- [ ] 1 teaspoon salt

Instructions

1. Prepare the rice by first washing it in a large pot with cold water. Rub the grains gently between your hands to loosen any starch, turning the water cloudy. Drain the rice well and rinse several times, until the water runs clear. Let drain for 30 minutes.

2. Add the rice to a wide pot or skillet and add the dashi, soy sauce, mirin, salt, and half the crab meat. Bring to a boil over high heat, then immediately turn heat down to low. Cook for 20 minutes, then turn the burner off and let sit on the warm stove for another 10–15 minutes.

3. When all the liquid has been absorbed, gently fold the rice with a spatula to fluff it up a bit, then mix in the remaining crab meat to serve.

CUCUMBER CRAB SALAD

Makes 4 servings

CUISINE NOTE: Typically this dish is served with the full crab, but I'm not one for shells in soups. Shelling the crabs and adding the meat to miso soup is my favorite way to serve it. You can also use imitation crab and skip the mess entirely.

COOKING TIP: Pickled cucumber is easy to make ahead of time, it's a staple in my fridge. Make a large batch of cucumber marinated in vinegar, then mix in the crab just before serving.

Ingredients

- [ ] 1 cucumber
- [ ] 1 teaspoon salt
- [ ] ½ cup crab meat
- [ ] 1 teaspoon sesame seeds, toasted
- [ ] ¼ cup sanbaizu vinegar (see recipe)

Instructions

1. Thinly slice the cucumber using a mandoline slicer, then place in a bowl with the salt and stir to combine. Let sit for 5 minutes, then rinse under cold water and gently squeeze the cucumber to get rid of any excess water.

2. Shred the crab meat, then mix with the cucumber. Add the sesame seeds and sanbaizu, then stir to combine. Let sit for 30 minutes to let flavors combine, then serve chilled.

FOOD WARS!: SHOKUGEKI NO SOMA

Growing up in his family's restaurant, Soma Yukihira wants nothing more than to become a full-time chef in the family business and surpass his father's culinary skills. But alas, his father suddenly decides to get a job requiring him to travel the world. They close down the shop, and instead of working in the restaurant, Soma finds himself enrolling in Totsuki Saryo Culinary Institute. This is no ordinary culinary school; students engage in food wars over anything from cooking utensils and titles to expulsion from school! Pressure's on, Soma! Learning that his father was in the elite top ten students during his time there, Soma sets off to become the best chef the school has ever seen. And with a whacky, creative flair, he just might achieve it!

Following this series, some of the recipes are delicious, some are a bit crazy, and some are downright genius! One dish in particular I just loved was his "Yukihira Style Char Okakiage," rice cracker breaded fish. With an assignment to create a dish using only ingredients on the premises, he finds a way to make a breaded fish when no other student ever had! A genius chef if ever there was one. Without flour, he turns to the next best thing: the bagged crackers of the supervising chef. And oh how I love rice crackers.

YUKIHIRA STYLE CHAR OKAKIAGE

Makes 4 servings

CUISINE NOTE: The unique sauce paired with the fish is called *tamago no moto*, a hard word to translate but basically means egg base. It's basically like a Japanese hollandaise sauce, but uses raw egg instead. Give it a shot, the creaminess is worth it!

COOKING TIP: The secret to a good coating is a fine line between too chunky and a thin powder. If the crackers are too big, they will fall off, but too small and you lose a bit of the crunchiness. Shake the bag a couple of times as you work to help the big pieces rise to the top. That makes it easier to know when to stop!

Ingredients

- [ ] 1 cup mixed rice crackers or pub mix
- [ ] 2 catfish filets
- [ ] 3 eggs, separated
- [ ] ½ teaspoon lemon juice
- [ ] 1 tablespoon miso
- [ ] ½ cup vegetable oil
- [ ] ½ teaspoon salt

Instructions

1. Mix the egg yolks and lemon juice with a beater in a small bowl. Continue to beat, adding in oil a few drops at a time until the sauce begins to thicken. Keep on adding the rest of the oil, then stir in the miso and salt. Set aside.

2. Prepare the breading by placing the rice crackers in a Ziploc bag. Using a dough roller or your hands, hit the bag a few times until the crackers have crumbled into small pieces. Place in a small plate, and place the egg whites in a small bowl.

3. Place about an inch of oil in a small frying pan and place over medium high heat. While the oil is heating up, bread the catfish by first patting dry with paper towels, then dip in the egg whites and immediately coating with the crackers.

4. When the oil is hot, add one catfish fillet at a time to the oil and fry for about 5 minutes a side, until golden brown. Transfer to paper towels and let sit a few minutes to remove excess oil.

5. Serve warm with dipping sauce on the side.

SHIROBAKO

Do you ever stop and think about all the work that actually goes into the anime we enjoy? It's no easy task, as five friends soon learn after forming an animation club in high school to take their passion further. After they proudly present their first amateur film at the school's yearly festival, they vow to pursue careers in the field and one day make their own show as a team again. Fast forward two years, and well, things aren't going as smoothly as they hoped. Two of them have managed to land jobs, but the others are still struggling to make it at all, quickly realizing that getting their dream job is not easy! These girls will learn that the path to success is far from smooth, but with perseverance and a touch of eccentric creativity, they may just make it!

Times may get tough, but donuts will get you through just about anything. And not just any donuts, Don Don Donuts! With a rallying cheer, "Don Don Donuts, let's go nuts!" the girls always manage to raise their spirits with a healthy dose of sugar. While regular donuts are a bit challenging to make, donut holes are super easy! These cakey donut holes are quick to make and even quicker to eat, getting you back to your anime binge ASAP!

OKINAWAN DONUTS (SATA ANDAGI)

Makes 4 servings

CUISINE NOTE: Unlike traditional donuts, with toppings sprinkled over them or piped into the middle, these donuts have the flavor mixed right into the dough, making them super easy to make. Classic flavors include sesame, sweet potato, chocolate, cinnamon, or matcha.

COOKING TIP: The donuts are almost too easy to cook, making them easy to burn! Keep the oil temperature low and only cook a few at a time, just in case the oil is too hot! If they start to burn too quickly, you can try salvaging them by removing them from the oil and baking them in the oven for about 5 minutes at 350 degrees Fahrenheit.

Ingredients

- 2 eggs
- ⅓ cup dark brown sugar
- 1 teaspoon oil
- 1 cup cake flour
- 1 teaspoon baking powder
- ¼ teaspoon salt
- 1 teaspoon flavoring, if desired
- Oil for frying

Instructions

1. In a large mixing bowl, whisk together the egg, sugar, and a teaspoon of oil. Sift cake flour, baking powder, and salt in a small bowl, then add to the egg mixture along with any flavoring desired. Let rest for one hour.

2. Add about 2 inches of oil into a small pot and place over a medium heat. While the oil is heating up, prepare the donuts by shaping a spoonfuls of dough into small balls, about 1 inch in diameter. Place on a lightly floured surface until ready to cook.

3. When the oil is hot, about 300 degrees Fahrenheit, place a few balls of dough at a time into the oil. Let fry until the balls start to float, stirring occasionally to let all sides brown evenly. When they float, remove from the oil with a slotted spoon and place on paper towels to drain. Continue frying until all donuts are cooked.

4. Serve hot, as is or dusted with powdered sugar.

K-ON!

Young, carefree Yui Hirasawa has her imagination captured when she sees a poster advertising the "Light Music Club" at school. It doesn't take long before she signs up; however, Yui has a bit of a problem—she can't play an instrument! While disappointed in lack of ability, they need the extra headcount to keep the club together! With boundless spunk and imagination, Yui is determined to be a valuable guitarist, one way or another. After all, with the support of good friends, and a good bit of dedication, anything is possible!

In the K-On! movie, Yui and the band visit a sushi-go-round during a visit in London—a delicious experience if you ever get the chance. When they enter the establishment, they're confronted by the manager and, as is only natural in a comedy, language barriers and cultural misunderstandings end up with them playing music for the restaurant patrons in a case of mistaken identity! Playing music while surrounded by tantalizingly delicious sushi...it must have been quite the performance! Making sushi can be an intimidating task: using a mat to roll it perfectly tight, forming little rice mounds just right, etc. It's no wonder that aspiring sushi chefs work for years before they're even allowed to touch the rice. Luckily, hand rolled sushi is a popular variety to make at home. All the deliciousness without the fuss!

HAND ROLLED SUSHI (TEMAKI)

Makes 4 servings

CUISINE NOTE: Homemade sushi uses a variety of serving techniques, such as serving it in a bowl with the toppings scattered across the top, called chirashi sushi, or making personal hand rolls by folding sheets of seaweed around ingredients as we do here. Easy to customize, and great for entertaining!

COOKING TIP: While we associate sushi with cold, the rice is actually room temperature. Chill the fillings in the fridge until ready to eat, but keep the rice on the counter to cool down. Otherwise, you'll have dense, hard rice, not at all fun to eat!

Ingredients

- 2 cups prepared sushi rice, see recipe
- 6 sheets toasted nori seaweed, cut into 4 smaller squares
- Soy sauce
- Wasabi paste
- Pickled ginger
- Fillings such as:
    - Cucumber
    - Carrot
    - Cooked crab meat, chilled
    - Cooked shrimp, chilled
    - Sliced ham
    - Canned tuna mixed with mayo
    - Sushi grade raw fish
    - Sliced cheese
    - Avocado
    - Wasabi paste

Instructions

1. Prepare your chosen fillings by cutting vegetables into thin strips, and chopping meats and softer items into large chunks. Arrange on a platter, alongside the prepared sushi rice and cut nori sheets.

2. Place small bowls of soy sauce near each diner, alongside a plate of wasabi and pickled ginger. Mix a dab of wasabi in the soy sauce for added heat if desired.

3. To assemble, grab a sheet of nori and place a spoonful of rice in the bottom corner. Add a small amount of various toppings toward the middle, then roll the nori around everything to form a cone. Eat immediately, dipping in the soy sauce as desired.

SCI-FI & SUPERNATURAL

A delicate balance of exotic and economical ingredients to make it through harsh journeys and trying times.

As far back as humans can remember, there have always been elements of the supernatural and fiction in our lore. Day to day life is hectic and stressful, it's only natural to wonder what else there could be, or what would happen if it fell apart. As some of Japan's strongest work, the science fiction realm covers everything from space battles and alternate realities to zombie apocalypses and desolate wastelands, with the most Japanese domain arguably being Mecha, the mechanical humanoid robots used in combat of various sorts. Popular in its own right since the '50s, Mecha really took off with the success of the Gundam series in the late '70s, dubbed the "Star Wars of Japan." In some sense, Mecha almost drove the spread of anime culture to other countries, with hungry audiences looking to fill the void while they waited for the next Star Wars film to be released. Ironically, without Star Wars, anime might not be what it is today! While Mecha may not make an appearance in all series, elements of robots often show, such as with the cybernetic humans found in Ghost in the Shell, and general space travel in the space western Cowboy Bebop.

In the supernatural domain, Japanese people are quite intrigued with the idea of supernatural elements just out of reach of their day to day life. The Shinto religion teaches several important things. One, that most things have a spirit, gods reside in trees and rivers all around, and they can be enticed to help us if we honor them. Two, our ancestors are still among us in some sense, so we must honor them after death, and death and ghosts are simply part of the natural order of things. And lastly, numerous yokai, or mythical demons, are just out of sight and interacting with us every day, so all sorts of day to day occurrences can be explained away by their mischievous acts. As a result, we see a unique flavor of supernatural fantasy in shows, ranging from yokai heavy stories, such as GeGeGe No Kitaro, or spiritual characters intermingling with mere mortals in titles like Bleach and Inuyasha, all amazing stories that are only made possible by the unique culture of Japan.

A UTILITARIAN FEAST

Luxury and famine are opposite sides of the same coin, so when starting this dish, take stock of your ingredients and build from there. Start with a utilitarian base, a simple palette with basic stock, and add flavor and nuance as the season allows. Is humanity in trying times, or in the midst of conflict? Choose your background and set the stage from there. Space travel or an alternate reality are an easy base, but on occasion even modern day Tokyo can work surprisingly well. Find a way to make it a bit unnatural though, otherwise you may end up with an everyday adventure. Pick one or two youthful characters to brighten the dish, but don't overdo it, since too much happiness can do more harm than good. Remember, this is a battle, so keep an air of somberness over the whole process.

Add depth and texture by creating a good dough, versatile in usage and also high in calories. Conflict is necessary, building structure and developing the gluten, so knead the dough thoroughly, but don't overdo it! A tough, chewy loaf consumes more energy than it yields.

Given the uncertainty of the times, take what you can get and waste nothing in the process! Leftovers from watching a character grow up? Toss it in for a little character development. A pile of vegetable scraps created after chiseling away a character's composure? Perfect for simmering in a good stock. A resourceful chef will excel in this environment, embodying the mantra: waste not, want not.

On occasion you may come across a rare delicacy, made extra special given the spartan times, so mix it in at the end. It's important to keep morale high if you hope for eventual success. Add just a little to stretch it out longer, for who knows how long it will be before you come across some again. Just before serving, place it over intense heat to really get the energy going, and just when it seems it's going to boil over: BAM! Toss it in, and serve immediately.

FULLMETAL ALCHEMIST

"Humankind cannot gain anything without first giving something in return. To obtain, something of equal value must be lost. That is alchemy's first law of Equivalent Exchange. In those days, we really believed that to be the world's one, and only truth." These words set a pair of brothers on a dark path neither of them could foresee. Set in a world where alchemy is very much real and its practice regulated by the government, a tragic loss drives the two orphaned Elric brothers make one very costly mistake, Edward losing a few limbs, Alphonse a whole lot more. Not to be discouraged, the pair set off to find the one thing that can restore their bodies, a philosopher's stone. The promise of infinite possibilities from the stone seems almost too good to be true, but everything comes at a cost. Little do they know the path to finding one is filled with secrets even darker!

We tend to think people would pursue the stone for greed, but the Elric brothers' could care less about that. While some alchemists are striving for fame and fortune, the brothers motivation is centered around one thing—family—which is why seeing them interacting with Lieutenant Hughes, who loves his family more than anything, is extra touching. I loved seeing them invited to the Hughes home and served a homemade meal. They get a little taste of everything they've been missing, which makes the quiche extra special: the secret ingredient is love!

SALTED SALMON QUICHE

Makes 8 servings

CUISINE NOTE: Japanese/Western fusion cuisine, called *washoku*, brings the best of both worlds together. The addition of salted salmon to this traditionally French dish makes this quiche extra special!

COOKING TIP: A soggy crust can easily ruin an otherwise amazing pie. While you can use the pie crusts as is, the filling needs a little less cooking time than the crust. Blind baking the crust before adding the filling helps give it a little more oven time, giving it a chance to get nice a flaky!

Ingredients

- [ ] 6 large eggs, beaten
- [ ] ½ cup heavy cream
- [ ] 1 tablespoon flour
- [ ] 1 cup chopped fresh spinach
- [ ] 2 tablespoons butter
- [ ] 1 small onion, chopped
- [ ] 1 pound salted salmon
- [ ] 1 cup mozzarella cheese
- [ ] 1 9-inch refrigerated pie crust
- [ ] ¼ teaspoon pepper

Instructions

1. Preheat the oven to 375 degrees Fahrenheit. Place the pie crust upside down on a baking sheet so the rim of the crust is actually on the bottom. Bake for 20 minutes, then remove and flip the crust over. Prick the bottom of the crust all over with a fork, then return to the oven, baking for an additional 15 minutes. Remove from the oven and set aside. Turn the heat down to 300 degrees Fahrenheit.

2. While the crust is baking, prepare the filling. Place a large skillet over medium high heat. Add the butter, and when melted, add the salmon skin side down and cook for about 8 minutes, until the skin is crispy. Flip the fillets over and cook an additional 8 minutes. Remove from the skillet and let cool.

3. Without cleaning the pan, add the chopped onion to the skillet and turn heat down to medium. Let cook for 10 minutes until softened. Remove from heat and let cool.

4. Whisk the eggs, milk, and flour together until well blended. Layer the spinach, onions, salmon, and cheese in the bottom of the pie crust, then pour the egg mixture on top. Bake for 45–50 minutes until the egg mixture is set. Let cool slightly before cutting.

SALTED SALMON

Makes 6 servings

CUISINE NOTE: Salted salmon is so ubiquitous in Japan people hardly make it themselves. The saltiness does wonders to the flavor! It can be served for breakfast or dinner as a fillet, crumbled up inside rice balls for a handy lunch, or even my personal favorite, served in a tea based rice soup called *ochazuke*.

COOKING TIP: For really good salted salmon pulling out moisture is key! It's traditionally made by hanging out in the breeze all winter to dry, but here we'll improvise. Use paper towels somewhat liberally, and let it sit for several days for the salt to bring out more flavor.

Ingredients

- 1 pound salmon
- ¼ cup sake
- 2 tablespoons salt

Instructions

1. Rinse salmon in cold water and pat dry. Cut lengthwise into 6–8 individual portions, then place in a shallow tray and pour the sake over the fillets. Let sit 10–20 minutes, then rinse and pat dry.

2. Spread the salt evenly over all sides of salmon, rubbing it into the surface. Prepare a Tupperware with some folded paper towels at the bottom, then sprinkle the bottom with a little extra salt. Place the salmon skin side down onto the paper towel, layering the fish between layers of paper towel sprinkled with salt as the container fills up. Let sit in the refrigerator for 2–3 days.

3. When the salmon feels almost rubbery from the water being pulled out, it's ready to go! Prepare it as you would regular salmon or store it for later by wrapping each piece tightly in plastic wrap before freezing.

ATTACK ON TITAN

No longer the top of the food chain, humanity has retreated inside enormous walls to protect themselves from man-eating titans roaming the land. Suddenly appearing about one hundred years earlier and exhibiting no clear motivations except the insatiable hunger to eat people, these enormous titans cannot easily be destroyed, merely avoided and contained. As long as the walls hold up, they're safe. Every defense has a weakness though, and one day a titan breaks through, plunging Eren Yeager and his friends into chaos as their world crumbles before them.

Humanity's last line of defense is the military, and Eren and his friends all join the Survey Corps to face the titans head on, but military life is quite hard. It's not without its benefits though—food is less scarce for them, since hungry soldiers are no good to anyone. Sasha in particular cherishes this perk, having lived with food insecurity her whole life, and never misses an opportunity to eat! Lined up in formation on her first day, she boldly eats a roasted potato while awaiting their daily instructions! Given that roasted potatoes are so delicious, can you really blame her?

ROASTED SWEET POTATOES (YAKIMO)

Makes 4 servings

CUISINE NOTE: Roasted sweet potatoes, called yaki imo, or yakimo for short, are a popular street food in colder months. Sold out of trucks, the vendor slow roasts the potatoes in a coal grill, enticing customers with the slow rhythmic singing of "yaaakiiimooo" throughout the streets.

COOKING TIP: You can use Western orange sweet potatoes, but if you can, splurge on a Japanese variety. Japanese sweet potatoes are dryer and a little nuttier in taste, with a yellow flesh and purple colored skin. If you really want to go all in, try mimicking the roasting process more by lining the bottom of the baking pan with some clean rocks. A little bit of gravel will do the trick!

Ingredients

- 4 sweet potatoes

Instructions

1. Preheat the oven to 300 degrees Fahrenheit. Wash the potatoes under running water, gently scrubbing the skin to remove any excess dirt. Wipe with paper towels and let dry completely.

2. Wrap each potato first with a paper towel, then with aluminum foil, sealing the potato in completely. Place on a baking sheet and bake in the oven for 2½ hours.

3. Turn the oven off but leave the potatoes inside to cool down for another 30 minutes.

4. Serve warmed. They are amazing as is, but you can sprinkle them with salt, top with a pat of butter, or even try a drizzle of honey!

CANDIED SWEET POTATOES (DAIGAKU IMO)

Makes 4 servings

CUISINE NOTE: In America, we have the cliche of college students eating instant ramen since it's cheap and filling. In Japan, the cliche is candied sweet potatoes instead. Cheap, filling, and heavy in carbs to keep your brain happy, it's perfect for late night cram sessions!

COOKING TIP: The angled cutting technique created by rotating the potatoes is called rangiri in Japanese. It's great for starchy root vegetables such as carrots. And adding just a dash of vinegar helps prevent the sugar from hardening.

Ingredients

- 4 sweet potatoes
- 3 tablespoons oil
- 4 tablespoons sugar
- ½ teaspoon soy sauce
- ¼ teaspoon rice vinegar
- 1 teaspoon roasted black sesame seeds

Instructions

1. Scrub the sweet potatoes gently under running water to remove any dirt, then pat dry with a paper towel.

2. Cut the potatoes at an angle into large chunks, turning the potato as you cut it to get angled edges. Place in a large bowl of cold water for 10 minutes to remove excess starch, then drain and pat dry.

3. Place a large skillet on the stove over medium heat. Add the oil, and when hot, add the sweet potato and fry for about 5 minutes, until the edges develop a light golden color.

4. Combine the sugar, soy sauce, and vinegar in a small bowl. Stir to combine, then add to the pan. Continue cooking the potatoes, stirring every 2 minutes so the sauce gets evenly soaked into the potatoes. Cook until just softened through, which, depending on the size of the chunks, should take about 5–7 minutes.

5. When cooked, remove from heat, sprinkle with sesame seeds, and serve. They're delicious hot or at room temperature.

STEINS;GATE

What would you do if you discovered time travel? Probably not get involved in murder and corporate corruption, but hey, when do things ever work out perfectly? Self-proclaimed mad scientist Okabe Rintarou lives in the otaku heaven, Akihabara, inventing "future gadgets" with his fellow lab members, all somewhat eclectic themselves. Through their experimentation process, they discovered the ability to time travel, but they aren't the only ones who have! A strange organization named SERN has been doing their own research, and are now on the hunt to track them down. Now it's a careful game of cat and mouse to not get caught and moreover, stay a step ahead in order to survive!

Dr. Pepper is available in Japan, but when you think of soft drinks, Coca Cola reigns supreme. That is, until Steins;Gate came on the scene. What else would a mad scientist drink but a drink for doctors? They don't call it Mr. Pepper, do they? An example of well placed advertisements, Dr. Pepper had a surge of popularity among otaku after the series was released, so in the otaku spirit, let's make a few Dr. Pepper inspired dishes.

DR. PEPPER BEEF AND POTATOES (NIKUJAGA)

Makes 4 servings

CUISINE NOTE: Traditionally this dish is sweetened with mirin, a sweet cooking wine. Here, we use Dr. Pepper instead, which is much easier to find in the grocery store. You can also try Coca Cola or Pepsi!

COOKING TIP: While it is a simmered dish, browning the meat is key to getting a deeper flavor profile. Just don't burn it in the process!

Ingredients

- [ ] 1 pound beef, cut into large chunks
- [ ] 1 large onion, sliced
- [ ] 2 cloves garlic, minced
- [ ] 4 small Yukon gold potatoes, cut into large chunks
- [ ] 2 carrots, cut into large chunks
- [ ] ½ cup sugar snap peas, cut into slices
- [ ] 3 cups dashi
- [ ] 2 tablespoons sugar
- [ ] 3 tablespoons Dr. Pepper
- [ ] 3 tablespoons soy sauce
- [ ] 3 tablespoons sake
- [ ] 1 tablespoon sesame oil
- [ ] Salt and pepper, to taste

Instructions

1. Heat a wide skillet over medium-high heat. Season the beef with salt and pepper, then add the oil to the pan and stir-fry the beef until a nice sear develops. Remove from the pan and set aside in a small bowl, leaving as much oil in the pot as possible.

2. Add onions and cook until translucent, about 6–8 minutes. Add garlic, potatoes and carrots and continue cooking for 3 minutes.

3. Add the sake and bring to a boil. Add the dashi, sugar, salt, soy sauce, and Dr. Pepper, then return the beef to the pot. Simmer partially covered on low heat for 30 minutes.

4. Add peas and cook uncovered until they are cooked through. Serve immediately.

DR. PEPPER CHOCOLATE CAKE

Makes 8 servings

Ingredients

- [ ] 3 egg whites
- [ ] 3 egg yolks
- [ ] ⅔ cup sugar
- [ ] ¾ cup cake flour, sifted
- [ ] ¼ cup Dr. Pepper
- [ ] 3 tablespoons butter, melted
- [ ] 3 tablespoons cocoa powder

Instructions

1. Prepare your baking pan by greasing the pan with oil, then lining with parchment paper.

2. Add the egg whites to a large mixing bowl, then using a mixer, beat on high until the egg whites are a smooth consistency. Add the sugar, and continue whipping for about 10–15 minutes until doubled in size and shiny. Once stiff peaks form when you lift the beaters, it is ready.

3. Mix the egg yolks until smooth, then mix in the butter and Dr.

Pepper. Using a spatula, gently fold the mixture into meringue, taking care not to stir and deflate the batter. Sift cake flour and chocolate together, then fold into the batter as well.

4. Pour the batter into the lined mold. Drop the filled cake pan a few times gently on the counter to remove any air pockets.

5. Bake for 30–40 minutes in a preheated 350 degree F oven, until a toothpick inserted in the middle comes out clean. Remove from the oven and cover with a kitchen towel to cool.

6. Once cool, take the cake out of the pan and remove the parchment paper.

CODE GEASS

Gundams and superpowers, a recipe for success! Set in an alternate world, the series follows the dashing Lelouch vi Britannia with a grudge to settle. Having lost his mother and retreating to Japan to keep him and his sister safe from the perils of court life, Lelouch decides to bring the Britannia Empire down when he receives the power of the Geass, allowing him to exert his will over others. But the clock is ticking, the more he uses it, the stronger it becomes. Will his power consume him before he pulls it off?

For a show that's not about food, there sure is a lot of pizza! Originally sponsored by Pizza Hut as a response to pizza advertising in Eureka 7 by a different pizza chain, what started off as a two to three appearance placement became revved up with the excitement of the production team, and I totally get where they're coming from! Pizza wars in anime...wonderful isn't it? Being a pizza lover, it's exciting to explore the Japanese take on an American comfort food. While of course you can't go wrong with a classic cheese or pepperoni pizza, try something new by adding in something a little more unusual!

OKARA PIZZA

Makes 1 pizza

CUISINE NOTE: Mayonnaise on pizza? Don't judge it until you try it! Japanese mayo tastes slightly different, but even your everyday mayo can be quite good. It's so popular Domino's Japan even lists mayo on its menu. Popular toppings also include teriyaki style chicken, corn, miso, seaweed, eggs, even hot dogs, (yes, sliced hot dogs!) though my favorite combo is mushrooms and green onions, with plenty of mozzarella and a sprinkling of furikake on top!

COOKING TIP: Don't have okara? No worries, it's just ground soybean pulp leftover from making soy milk (see the soy milk recipe). You can grind up your own in a food processor, or just leave it out and use another ½ cup flour. Okara is a great way to sneak in a little extra protein, so if you're looking for a way to make you pizza a bit healthier, give it a try!

Ingredients

- 2¼ teaspoons active dry yeast (1 package)
- 2 tablespoons honey
- 1 cup warm water
- 2½ cups all-purpose flour
- ½ cup dried okara
- 1 teaspoon salt
- 2 tablespoons oil
- 2 tablespoons cornmeal
- Sauce and toppings as desired

Instructions

1. Dissolve the yeast and honey in the warm water in a large bowl or stand mixer. Add the flour, okara, salt, and oil and mix well, adding in ¼ cup or so of water if needed to form a sticky ball. Knead for 15 minutes until the dough becomes smooth and elastic.

2. Place the dough in a greased bowl and turn over to grease the top. Cover and let rise until doubled in a warm place for about 45 minutes.

3. Punch down the dough and divide into two balls. Wrap tightly and refrigerate for up to two days before using.

4. To bake, sprinkle cornmeal on a greased cookie sheet or pizza stone and stretch the dough out to the desired thinness. Top with desired ingredients and bake at 425 degrees Fahrenheit for 15–20 minutes.

QUICK AND EASY PIZZA SAUCE

Makes 2½ cups

Ingredients

- 1 15-ounce can tomato sauce
- 1 6-ounce can tomato paste
- 2 cloves garlic, crushed
- 1 teaspoon dried oregano
- 1 teaspoon dried basil
- ⅛ teaspoon red pepper flakes
- 1 tablespoon honey
- 2 tablespoons grated parmesan cheese

Instructions

1. Combine the tomato sauce and tomato paste until combined and smooth. Add remaining ingredients and stir well to combine. Let sit for 30 minutes before using for the flavors to combine.

COWBOY BEBOP

While they may be fighting crime, the Bebop team are far from superheroes. Intergalactic bounty hunters out to make a buck, this motley crew of misfits find there's strength in numbers as they work together to go after the big bucks. The muscle, Spike, is a hero whose cool façade hides a dark and deadly past. The pilot, Jet, is a restless scoundrel who can't wait to collect the next bounty. The femme fatale, Faye Valentine, is prone to breaking hearts and separating fools from their money. And of course we can't forget the support team! Along for the ride is the strangely brilliant computer hacker Ed, whose skills come in handy, and the adorable super Corgi, Ein.

Being bounty hunters, they don't really operate on a fixed salary. Sometimes the money's good, sometimes not so good, but they learn to take it in stride. We see some of the not so good right in the first episode, where they feast on a beef and pepper stir fry. Classic bachelor chow, super easy to make. But money's tight, so alas, there's no beef! Of course, if you can afford beef, don't be afraid to splurge!

BEEF AND PEPPER STIR FRY

Makes 4 servings

CUISINE NOTE: When it comes to stir fry, you don't need a set recipe. It's a great way to use up whatever is in the fridge, just take whatever vegetables and meats you see and slice them up! To make it more Chinese in spirit, you can add in some oyster sauce to the pan towards the end, but here I just use Japanese flavors.

COOKING TIP: A good stir fry is quick to cook, resulting in a satisfying crispness in texture. Cook the vegetables just enough to soften, but not until they wilt.

Ingredients

- ▢ 1 pound beef, thinly sliced
- ▢ 2 green bell peppers, deseeded and thinly sliced
- ▢ 1 onion, thinly sliced
- ▢ 2 cloves garlic, minced
- ▢ ½ inch fresh ginger, grated
- ▢ 2 tablespoons soy sauce
- ▢ 2 tablespoons sesame oil
- ▢ Salt and pepper, to taste

Instructions

1. Place a wide skillet over medium high heat. Once hot, add the sesame oil, garlic, and ginger and stir until fragrant. Add the beef and let cook 5–6 minutes until the edges start to sear.

2. Add the vegetables and cook another 3–4 minutes until they start to soften. Add the soy sauce, salt and pepper, and stir to coat. Remove from heat and serve alongside steamed rice.

DEATH PARADE

When we die, we expect to either go to heaven or hell. But what if you found yourself somewhere else? For some unlucky souls, at the instant of their death, they arrive at the Quindecim, a strangely empty bar attended by the mysterious white-haired Decim. Along with your choice of drinks, he also serves you a chance to win. Win what? We'll get to that later. The catch is, you cannot leave until the game is over one way or another, and when it is your life may be, too. What's the game? Well, that would ruin the surprise!

It can't be easy to process the news that you've died. It's a good thing they find themselves at a bar! A little alcohol might ease the shock, at least until they discover the next shock, where they spend eternity depends entirely on how well they play the game set before them. Maybe a little alcohol will help them play a little better. At the very least, savor the drink while it lasts! While you can't go wrong with sake, here are a few cocktails to enjoy.

MATCHA HIGHBALL

Makes 1 serving

CUISINE NOTE: In Japan, two drinks reign supreme: Japanese whisky and matcha tea. Try this combination with your favorite whiskey, American or Japanese. Jack Daniels is an excellent choice, and is quite well known in Japan!

COOKING TIP: To improve the color and reduce clumping, it's best to let the matcha steep in the whisky for a little bit, but if you're in a hurry, you can just shake it and serve! If you really like the drink, you can prep a whole bottle of whiskey ahead of time to have on hand.

Ingredients

- [ ] 2 oz whiskey
- [ ] 4 oz club soda
- [ ] 1 teaspoon matcha powder
- [ ] Cubed ice

Instructions

1. Rinse a highball glass under cold water and place in the freezer for a few minutes to chill. Combine the whiskey and matcha in a cocktail shaker and shake to combine. Let sit for at least 30 minutes to let flavors combine.

2. Take the glass out of the freezer and add as much ice as desired. Pour in the club soda, then slowly pour the whisky on top. Serve layered, or serve to combine.

CRANBERRY UMETINI

Makes 1 serving

CUISINE NOTE: Plum wine, or *umeshu*, is another common alcoholic beverage in Japan. Delightfully sweet, it is delicious as it is or mixed in other drinks.

COOKING TIP: I typically pair umeshu with sweet things, but pickled plums, called *umeboshi*, are deliciously sour. If you enjoy a traditional martini, try mixing plum wine with pickled plums and skip the cranberry juice...just be sure to remove the pits!

Ingredients

- [ ] 4 oz plum wine
- [ ] 2 oz dry gin
- [ ] 2 oz cranberry juice
- [ ] 1 Maraschino cherry

Instructions

1. Rinse a martini glass under cold water and place in the freezer for a few minutes to chill.

2. Mix all the ingredients in a cocktail shaker filled with ice. Pour the ingredients out into the chilled martini glass. Serve as is or garnished with a cherry.

SPICY EDAMAME

Makes 2 servings

CUISINE NOTE: Across the world, cultures have their standard snacks to pair with drinking. Called *otsumami* in Japanese, they include a wide range of dishes from rice cracker pub mixes to all varieties of pickles. But my favorite, and easiest to make, is shelled edamame!

COOKING TIP: Edamame is easy to cook and excellent served plain, but adding seasoning makes it more fun! First the spicy flavor hits your lips, then a bean pops into your mouth, it's a double hit! You can also make these ahead of time and let the flavor penetrate the shell instead...but it's hard to wait that long!

Ingredients

- ½ pound frozen edamame
- 2 tablespoons sesame oil
- 1 clove garlic, minced
- 1 teaspoon chili paste
- 1 teaspoon salt
- Red pepper flakes, for garnish

Instructions

Prepare the edamame according to package instructions, then set aside.

Heat the oil in a small frying pan over medium heat. When the pan is hot, add the garlic and chili paste and cook for one minute. Add in the edamame and salt, and stir until well coated. Transfer to serving bowls, then sprinkle with red pepper flakes to serve.

GEGEGE NO KITARÕ

In the modern world of science and reason, most people have relegated folklore to the realm of fantasy. Twenty-first century Tokyoites have nearly forgotten the existence of yokai, the mythical creatures that range from friendly to harmful, but a good deal downright mischievous. When a number of strange things suddenly start plaguing the human world, thirteen-year-old Mana writes a letter to the Yokai Post in search of answers, only to be greeted by GeGeGe no Kitarō himself. Being the last surviving member of the Ghost Tribe, a group of yokai charged with keeping the peace between yokai and humanity, it's Kitaro's job to save the day, which means he's got his work cut out for him!

Being a cherished series since the 1960's, Kitaro is so popular partly because it exposes us to unique Japanese folklore that's been all but forgotten in the modern age. Kitaro crosses paths with a variety of creatures, ghosts, and gods in his attempts to help humans, bringing exposure to all-but-forgotten mythical creatures. For example, in one episode, turtle-like river dwellers called kappa are tricked into working as salarymen under a greedy businessman. What would ever motivate them to do such a crazy thing? A salary paid in cucumbers! Being their favorite food, a couple of cucumbers is quite the deal for them, at least for a little while. And given the amazing variety of Japanese dishes using cucumbers, can you really blame them for falling for it?!

JAPANESE CUCUMBER SALAD (SUNOMONO)

Makes 4 servings

CUISINE NOTE: *Sunomono* belongs to a category of food called *namazu*, which are vegetables dressed in vinegar. Cucumbers and vinegar pair wonderfully together, but vinegared root vegetables offer a delightful crunch, especially if you let it marinate a bit!

COOKING TIP: All you really need is cucumbers and vinegar, but to add some variation, you can try adding parboiled octopus or crab legs. Toasted seeds are essential for getting a strong sesame flavor, but to kick it up a notch, add a teaspoon of sesame oil as well.

Ingredients

- [ ] 2 cucumbers
- [ ] 1 tablespoon dried wakame seaweed (optional)
- [ ] 1 teaspoon salt
- [ ] 4 tablespoons rice vinegar
- [ ] 2 tablespoons sugar
- [ ] 1 teaspoon soy sauce
- [ ] 1 tablespoon toasted sesame seeds

Instructions

1. Prepare the dressing by combining the rice vinegar, sugar, and soy sauce in a small bowl, then setting it aside for the flavors to combine.

2. If using wakame seaweed, place the dried seaweed in water and let it rehydrate for about 10 minutes.

3. Meanwhile, slice the cucumbers thinly into rounds. Sprinkle them with salt, gently rubbing them against each other to spread the salt across the surface. Set aside for 5 minutes.

4. Squeeze out as much water as you can from the seaweed and cucumber. Place them into the bowl with seasoning and coat well. Sprinkle with sesame seeds and serve. They're delicious chilled or at room temperature.

SLICE OF LIFE

Simple, delightful pleasures to remind you to pause and savor the moment every once in a while.

Not a well-known genre by name, elements of slice of life are seen all over anime. Almost reminiscent of reality TV, yet not quite so real, slice of life is a unique genre embodying many Japanese values, which is probably why it is so popular! If you want to understand Japanese culture a little more intimately, digging into slice of life is a great place to start.

While it may seem like another term for melodrama, slice of life really focuses more on the day to day interactions and situations of the characters. Plot development is deemphasized in order to focus more on the present moment, emphasizing seasonality, relationships, and everyday actions. Japanese tend to value feeling and emotion in how they view many aspects of life, from their decision making to just general outlook, which really plays into the slice of life story. Instead of focusing on progression, it focuses on being present, just embracing what is, and going with the flow. The story runs at a slower pace, but in some sense that slowness is refreshing!

Sometimes focusing on a rural setting, other times centered around school life, slice of life can be seen in many situations. With such diverse options, it's no wonder titles like Clannad, ReLIFE, Sayonara, Zetsubou-Sensei, Silver Spoon, Barakamon, and even My Neighbor Totoro are all great examples. As long as it's giving you a view of the day to day life of the characters, you've got a slice of life!

A PERFECT SLICE OF LIFE

Slice of life is a dish felt in the heart instead of experienced in the mind. While crafting this nourishing dish, keep feeling at the forefront of every decision and you'll be pleased with the results. Start with a relatable lead character. Choose one exhibiting youthful energy and one or two endearing character flaws—too many and it will overwhelm the senses. A good coming of age story does wonders to re-energize a tired body.

Throw in an everyday setting. A school typically works well, but others can bring out very delightful flavor, such as a business or a small rural town. For texture, choose from topics surrounding interpersonal relationships, family, self-development, or romance. Two or three should be plenty, otherwise the pan quickly becomes overcrowded.

Layer everything delicately in a large pot, then let it simmer nice and slow over low heat. A slower pace will help tenderize the meat, bringing out the natural sweetness. Resist the urge to stir too much, otherwise the dish might become excessively dramatic.

As the dish progresses, through in an occasional pop of flavor, such as a surprise visitor, or maybe an unexpected conflict. Nothing too potent, just enough to shock the senses a bit. When a pleasant aroma fills the kitchen, it's ready to serve. Melt in your mouth perfection!

BARAKAMON

With a unique title translating to "Energetic One," the story follows a talented young calligrapher Seishuu Handa going through a rough patch in his career. Wondering if he has lost his touch, he retreats to a rural village to find his purpose again. While settling in to his new home, he comes across an energetic girl, Naru Kotoishi, who uses the house as her hideout, and a beautiful friendship blossoms. Naru pushes him to get out of his shell and interact with the village, and Seishu is able to find some peace and clarity along the way. Which just goes to show, there's nothing quite like a country retreat to help find yourself!

In one episode, Seishu is handed a bag of homemade pickles, called *tsukemono*, from the house's caretaker. He receives it a little grudgingly, wondering what he's going to do with a huge bag of pickles, but if you've ever been in the countryside, you know how delicious fresh, homemade food can be! Of course, he takes a bite, and before he knows it, the whole bag is gone! Since tsukemono are so essential to Japanese food, I found the gesture quite profound, almost as if by eating the goodness of the tsukemono, it was in turn helping heal his soul.

TSUKEMONO SAMPLER

CUISINE NOTE: Japanese pickles come in many varieties, typically made using either salt, soy sauce, vinegar, miso, rice bran, or sake lees. The rice bran and sake lees varieties in particular can take months, but these recipes below use a quick pickling method to create crunchy, flavorful pickles in less than a day.

COOKING TIP: To get that wonderful crunch, it's important to draw out the water using salt. Lightly salting the vegetables at the beginning helps speed up the pickling process, giving you quicker pickles much faster!

QUICK PICKLED CABBAGE

Ingredients

- [ ] 1 small head napa cabbage, cut into 1 inch rounds
- [ ] 2 tablespoons salt
- [ ] 1 teaspoon instant dashi granules
- [ ] 1 tablespoon sesame oil
- [ ] 1 tablespoon red pepper

Instructions

1. Rinse the cabbage, then place in a Ziplock bag with the salt. Seal tightly, removing excess air, then gently massage the leaves for about 5 minutes, spreading the salt evenly among the leaves. Let the bag sit for about 30 minutes until the cabbage has released some water.

2. Open the bag and carefully drain the water, gently squeezing to release as much water as possible. Add the remaining ingredients, then close the bag and massage the cabbage again to distribute the flavor. Place in the refrigerator and let sit for at least an hour before serving.

SOY SAUCE PICKLED MUSHROOMS

Ingredients

- [ ] 8 oz dried shiitake mushrooms
- [ ] 6 tablespoons sugar
- [ ] 4 tablespoons soy sauce
- [ ] 4 tablespoons rice vinegar
- [ ] 1 clove garlic, minced
- [ ] 1 inch fresh ginger, peeled and roughly chopped

Instructions

1. Steep the dried shiitakes in hot water for 30 minutes to soften. Strain the mushrooms, reserving 1 cup of the liquid. Remove the stems from the caps, slicing the caps thinly and discarding the stems.

2. Place remaining ingredients in a small pan along with 1 cup of the mushroom liquid and bring to a simmer over low heat. Cover and let for 20 minutes, then strain to remove the garlic and ginger.

3. Place the mushrooms in a small container, then pour the soy sauce mixture on top. Cover and refrigerate overnight before serving.

VINEGARED PICKLES

Ingredients

- [ ] 1 cucumber, thinly sliced
- [ ] 1 teaspoon salt
- [ ] 1 inch ginger, peeled, thinly sliced
- [ ] ¼ cup rice vinegar
- [ ] 1 tablespoon sugar

Instructions

1. Mix the cucumber with the salt in a small bowl. Let sit for 15 minutes to let some water draw out.

2. Combine vinegar and sugar in a small pan. Bring to a simmer over medium heat, stirring to dissolve the sugar. Once the sugar has completely dissolved, remove from heat and let cool.

3. Taking a handful at a time, gently squeeze the cucumber to draw out excess water. Place in a small lidded container, then pour the vinegar mixture on top. Shake gently to distribute the liquid evenly, then place in the refrigerator and let sit for at least a day before serving.

TORADORA

A kind heart hidden underneath an intimidating exterior, Ryuji Takasu is trying to put his best face forward entering his second year of high school. A difficult task, made even more difficult when he crosses paths with Taiga Aisaka, a tiny girl overflowing with rage. What starts out as an intense rivalry soon becomes a mutually beneficial friendship as the two help each other open up to others. Can they learn to be more friendly and open up to their crushes? It won't be easy, but love can find a way!

Taiga quickly finds herself joining in on the Takasu family meals, Ryuji being a talented cook and taking care of his working mom. At one point, Ryuji describes beans as "the meat you grow in your garden," and that is such a beautiful philosophy! A take on "waste not, want not", soybeans in Japan are used to make sauces, numerous tofu products, miso, milk…even just as edamame, they're everywhere! It's not hard to make a balanced meal featuring soy in every dish. In one episode, he makes his mom soy milk, a secret recipe to help her keep her womanly figure, and as many of us girls can relate, Taiga is instantly intrigued! Whether or not the isoflavones in soy is helpful in that regard, fresh soy milk is delicious and surprisingly straightforward to make.

FRESH SOY MILK

Makes 8 cups

CUISINE NOTE: Don't throw that soybean pulp away after you're done! Called *okara*, it can be used in a variety of ways. Spread it out on a baking pan and place in the oven at 250 degrees Fahrenheit until it dries out a bit, then you can mix it into doughs, meatloaves, smoothies, anywhere you want an extra dose of protein!

COOKING TIP: Caution, that pot will boil! The beans get very foamy, especially the first few minutes, so if you're not paying attention, it can boil over. Get the biggest pot you can find and watch the temperature, turning it down if it gets too hot.

Ingredients

- ☐ 1 cup dried soybeans
- ☐ 8 cups water, divided
- ☐ Sugar to taste, optional

Instructions

1. Place the soybeans in a large bowl and add enough water to cover. Let the beans soak overnight. Discard the water and rinse the beans.

2. Place the beans and 2 cups of water into a food processor. Blend until a thick paste forms.

3. Place a large pot with 3 cups of water over high heat. Add the bean paste and bring just to a boil, stirring occasionally. Reduce heat to medium and let simmer for 20 minutes. It will start to foam and bubble like crazy, so stay with it and keep stirring, skimming off the top foam as needed.

4. While the beans are simmering, place a large colander over a large bowl and line with cheesecloth. Once the beans have simmered, pour into the lined colander, emptying out the pot. Let the liquid drain off, gathering the cheesecloth around the pulp to squeeze out excess moisture.

5. Once drained, return the liquid to the pot and add an additional 3 cups of water. Simmer for another 10 minutes to remove the bitter flavor, adding sugar or other flavoring as desired.

RECOVERY OF AN MMO JUNKIE

Moriko Morioka was on a normal path in life. However, corporate life in Japan is tough, and at thirty years old, she has had enough! Instead, she decides to quit and become a neet (not in education, employment, or training), holed up in her apartment, diving into the online world. After joining an online game, she takes on the alter male ego Hayashi as her avatar. In the game, Hayashi meets another character Lily, a high-level player who takes him under her wing. Through the game she is able to make deeper friendships than she ever could in the real world, but the real world won't quite let her go. After a chance encounter with a handsome salary man Yuta Sakurai, she might not be able to remain a neet forever!

What's great about the show is how it portrays just how convenient a Japanese convenience store is. Living in a tiny apartment, there's not much of a kitchen, so Moriko depends quite heavily on convenience store food to survive in her reclusive lifestyle. Even though they have a wide variety of prepared foods, it's got to get tiring after a while. Just imagine the joy she feels when she sees the last piece of fried chicken in the counter display, only to end up fighting with another customer over who gets it! A recipe for disaster for someone looking to avoid people!

JAPANESE STYLE FRIED CHICKEN (CHICKEN KARAAGE)

Makes 4 servings

CUISINE NOTE: Fried chicken just so happens to be a popular Christmas meal in Japan! With a shortage of turkeys in Japan, KFC started marketing their chicken to homesick expats during the holiday season, and it soon became a nationwide trend.

COOKING TIP: To get really crispy chicken, fry the chicken twice! The first time seals in moisture to keep the inside juicy, the second time at a higher heat to get a delightful crunchy exterior.

Ingredients

- [ ] 1 pound chicken thigh fillets, cut into large bite sized pieces
- [ ] 1 tablespoon soy sauce
- [ ] 1 tablespoon sake
- [ ] 1 teaspoon mirin
- [ ] 1 inch ginger, grated
- [ ] 2 cloves garlic, minced
- [ ] 1 teaspoon salt
- [ ] ½ cup cornstarch
- [ ] Vegetable oil, for frying
- [ ] Lemon juice, for dipping
- [ ] Mayonnaise, for dipping

Instructions

1. Pat chicken dry with a paper towel. Mix together the soy sauce, sake, mirin, ginger, garlic, and salt, and place in a large plastic bag with the chicken. Seal tightly, then let marinate in the refrigerator for at least an hour, up to 4 hours.

2. Drain the excess marinade from the chicken, then pat dry with paper towels. Place cornstarch in another plastic bag, then add chicken, seal the bag, then toss around to coat the pieces evenly.

3. To prepare for frying, heat about 1½ inches of oil in a deep pot to 325 degrees Fahrenheit. When hot, work in small batches, adding a few pieces of chicken to the oil at a time. Fry each batch for 3 minutes, then remove from oil and let the chicken rest for at least 5 minutes. Once all the chicken has been fried, bring the oil temperature up to 375 degrees, and repeat frying in batches for another 3 minutes per batch. Remove from oil and drain thoroughly.

4. Serve with lemon and mayonnaise on the side.

POCO'S UDON WORLD

Like many Japanese youths, Souta Tawara dreamed of leaving his boring country life and heading to the glamour of Tokyo. Avoiding his complicated family relationship, he shuts down his feelings to escape to the city. His plans work for a while, until the death of his father forces him to return home. Of course, he tells himself it's only temporarily, he can't bear to stay in his hometown too long. But you can't escape your past forever, and he soon learns a quick trip won't quite cut it. Upon walking into the recently closed family udon shop, he finds a little boy sleeping in a cooking pot! What to do, what to do...

Souta quickly discovers that this is no normal little boy, but rather a magical tanuki disguised in human form! Naming him Poco and taking him under his wing, Souta quickly forms a bond that both desperately needed. Serving as a parental figure to Poco helps Souta work through his issues with his own late father, and while he may not want to re-open his father's udon shop, he finds a deeper appreciation for the life he left behind.

TANUKI UDON

Makes 4 servings

CUISINE NOTE: Tanuki are animals native to Japan that look a little like racoons. They have a colorful history in folklore, and are known as shapeshifters and tricksters. The dish gets its name from the deep color of the tempura flakes, which was said to remind people of a tanuki's fur.

COOKING TIP: Make sure those green onions are fresh! With so few ingredients, freshness is key for flavor, and old green onions have a very noticeable taste!

Ingredients

- [ ] 6 cups dashi
- [ ] 3 tablespoons mirin
- [ ] 3 tablespoons soy sauce
- [ ] 1½ tablespoons sugar
- [ ] 4 servings udon, cooked
- [ ] 4 green onions, thinly sliced
- [ ] 1 cup tempura flakes

Instructions

1. Combine the dashi, mirin, soy sauce, and sugar in a large pot. Bring to a boil, then let simmer 5 minutes.

2. To serve, place the udon in serving bowls, then ladle the hot broth on top. Sprinkle green onion and tempura flakes on top, then serve immediately.

FRESH HANDMADE UDON

Makes 4 servings

CUISINE NOTE: Udon is a very thick, chewy type of noodle, making it excellent for soups. It's served with broth and a variety of toppings, the simplest being a dish called *kake udon*, which just adds a little shredded green onions on top.

COOKING TIP: Kneading by hand can be exhausting. If you get tired, do what Japanese housewives do, use your feet! Place the dough in a large plastic bag, press out as much air as you can, then wrap the bag with a towel and stand on it, shifting your weight from foot to foot.

Ingredients:

- [ ] 3½ cups all-purpose flour
- [ ] 2 teaspoons salt
- [ ] 1 cup water

Instructions

1. Combine the flour, salt, and water in a large mixing bowl. Use your hands to mix until the dough starts to come together into a loose ball. Add a little water as needed until all the flour is incorporated into the dough.

2. Place the dough on a lightly floured surface and knead the dough for about 5 minutes until it feels smooth. Roll into a ball, cover in plastic wrap, and let sit at room temperature for 1–6 hours. The longer it sits, the more relaxed it becomes, making it easier to work with.

3. When ready to cut, knead the dough again on a lightly floured surface, then divide into 4 balls. Working with one ball at a time, use a rolling pin to roll out the dough into a rectangle, dusting with flour as needed for it to remain workable. Roll out to ¼ inch thickness, then let rest another 10 minutes.

4. Fold the sheet of dough over into thirds, as if folding a letter, then slice along the width to ⅛ inch thick noodles. Sprinkle with flour, then gently separate with your hands.

5. Bring a large pot of water to a boil, then add the cut udon. Cook for 8–10 minutes, then drain.

SILVER SPOON

Hachiken Yuugo is at a loss as to what to do with his future. Attending a tough prep school, studying all night, pushing himself to perform well on tests, and for what? So he can get into a fancy college and do more of the same, then get a position in a respectable company and work his life away as a salaryman?! No thank you. Seeing the unhappy path his father took, he enrolls in Oezo Agricultural High School, partly as an act of rebellion, and partly because it was something new. Interacting with farm kids working towards a variety of agricultural careers, Hachiken learns there's a lot more to life than he previously thought. He might not know where he's headed just yet, but so much work goes into the food on his plate, and that knowledge is enough to get him started.

At one point, Hachiken learns the hard way what many children learn on the farm, don't name the livestock! After interacting with a litter of piglets and noticing the runt struggling to eat, he finds himself quickly forming a bond with the adorable pig he names "Pork Bowl." While caring for him, Hachiken has to come to terms with the fact that one day Pork Bowl will be food. Can he accept that? Spoiler alert, there is some delicious bacon in his future!

BACON FRIED RICE

Makes 4 servings

CUISINE NOTE: Fried rice is typically called chahan in Japanese, but can also be called *yakimeshi*. There is no set recipe, you just need a protein such as pork or shrimp, an aromatic such as garlic or onions, a few vegetables, and an egg.

COOKING TIP: If you want to use leftover rice, make sure it's warmed up before adding it to the skillet. Cold rice takes longer to soften up, and since this dish it meant to be cooked quickly, it can ruin the texture of the other ingredients. Microwave it for about a minute and you're all set!

Ingredients

- ☐ 2 cups freshly cooked short grain rice
- ☐ 1 tablespoon sesame oil
- ☐ 2 cloves garlic, minced
- ☐ 1 large egg, whisked
- ☐ 4 slices bacon, chopped
- ☐ 2 green onions, chopped
- ☐ ¼ cup carrot, diced
- ☐ ¼ cup peas
- ☐ 1 tablespoon soy sauce
- ☐ Salt and pepper, to taste

Instructions

1. Take the freshly cooked rice and spread it out on a cutting board to cool to room temperature.

2. Place a wide skillet on the stove over medium heat. When hot, add bacon and cook until browned. Drain most of the fat from the pan, then return to the stove.

3. Add garlic to the pan. When fragrant, add the carrot and let cook 2–3 minutes until the carrot has softened. Add peas and green onion and cook one minute more.

4. Use a spatula to move the ingredients to the side, then add the egg to the pan. Stirring constantly, cook until firm, then move to the side of the pan as well.

5. Add sesame oil to the pan, then add the rice. Stir until warmed, and once the rice is no longer clumping together, add the soy sauce and stir to combine. Season with salt and pepper.

6. Serve with additional soy sauce on the side.

GOURMET GIRL GRAFFITI

After her grandmother passes away, middle schooler Ryo Machiko finds herself in Tokyo living on her own. A hard life for most adults, let alone a student, Ryo finds comfort in cooking, making dishes her grandmother used to make. But they just don't taste the same, and she can't quite figure out what's missing. When her cousin Kirin Morino comes from the country to attend an art school in Tokyo, Ryo discovers the missing ingredient: good company makes everything taste better! Through food, Ryo brings people together, making new friendships with classmates and exploring what dishes bring people happiness.

Being a student, there is a lot of pressure to study hard, get good grades, be at the top of the class, and all that stress. Summertime fun can sometimes be overlooked, and Ryo realizes this as they study their summer away diligently. In an attempt to embrace the summer while they still can, they come together to squeeze every summer activity they can in a single day. And what are some of the best activities? Food! One special dish they enjoy together is chilled somen noodles, served by sending the noodles down a bamboo pipe. A memorable experience for sure, but you can enjoy somen much more simply in your own kitchen. All you need is a little chilled water and you're all set.

CHILLED SOMEN

Makes 2 servings

CUISINE NOTE: There are restaurants in Japan that serve cold somen through bamboo slides as a dish called *nagashi somen.* Little portions are measured out at the top and customers sit along the long bamboo pipes and pick them up as they pass. If you want to be authentic, you can buy a tabletop bamboo somen slide on Amazon! But a simple chilled bowl served in front of you is just as delicious, if not a little less fun.

COOKING TIP: Somen is very thin so it cooks very quickly! Cook it quickly in hot water, then immediately transfer if to cold water so the noodles don't keep cooking and become soggy.

Ingredients

- ☐ 2 servings dried somen noodles
- ☐ 2 green onions, thinly sliced
- ☐ Sesame sauce (goma dare) for dipping, see recipe

Instructions

1. Bring a small pot of water to a boil. Add the somen and cook for one minute until softened. Drain immediately, then place under cold water to cool the noodles.

2. Place a small amount of ice water in serving bowls, then add the somen. Serve immediately alongside sliced green onion and little bowls of sesame sauce.

LUCKY STAR

Ever find yourself so bored you start asking the real questions about life? Like, what type of guy is really into a moe girl? Forget school work, these are the questions that need answers! Or at least, that's what the easily-bored Konata Izumi thinks. The uber otaku with a very inquisitive mind, Konata's laidback attitude never fails to frustrate the hard-working Kagami Hiiragi. And if their personalities aren't entertaining enough, the laid-back Tsukasa Hiiragi is adorably unreliable, while the high strung Miyuki Takara is concerned with propriety and order. A colorful mishmash of personalities and anime stereotypes, join these four friends as they navigate through everyday life.

As you might expect, these friends are entertaining right from the start. In the very first scene, we come face to face with Konata's inquisitive mind: how do you eat a chocolate cream horn? From the top, or the bottom? Which is the top and the bottom? Everyone has an opinion to share, as they very promptly do. As everyone weighs in on the topic, you start to wonder, just what type of show have you gotten yourself into?! Don't question it, just watch. And eat your own cream horn while you're at it, whichever way you prefer!

CHOCOLATE CREAM HORNS

Makes 8 servings

CUISINE NOTE: Not quite Japanese in origin, there are a variety of European style sweets in Japanese bakeries. Light, fluffy cakes and pastries are very popular all over the world!

COOKING TIP: Making these ahead of time? If you're worried your homemade whipped cream will lose its shape as it sits, add in about ¼ teaspoon of gelatin powder when you add in the chocolate. It will give it just enough firmness to keep it stiff, but not too stiff.

Ingredients

- [ ] 1 sheet frozen puff pastry dough
- [ ] 1 large egg, lightly beaten
- [ ] ⅓ cup heavy cream
- [ ] 2 tablespoons confectioners' sugar
- [ ] 1 tablespoon chocolate powder

Instructions

1. Thaw out the puff pastry in the fridge until it's soft enough to unfold. Fold it out onto a lightly floured surface, then cut the dough lengthwise into 8 long strips.

2. Working with one strip at a time, roll the strip around the horn mold, starting at the tip of the mold, overlapping the dough spiral about ⅛ of an inch on the previous spirals as you go. Press the dough into itself as you work to make it stick, and when you reach the end of the strip, tuck the end into the top of the spiral. Repeat with the remaining dough, then cover in plastic wrap and place in the fridge for at least 30 minutes.

3. Preheat the oven to 425 degrees. Brush the top of the dough with the egg. Bake for 12 minutes until golden brown, then remove the horns from the oven. Turn the oven heat down to 350 degrees Fahrenheit, then carefully remove the horns from the molds. Return to the oven for another 8–10 minutes until the insides are lightly browned. Remove from the oven and let cool completely.

4. Add the heavy whipping cream and sugar in a chilled metal bowl. Using an electric mixer to whip the cream to soft peaks. Add the chocolate, then continue beating with an electric mixer until stiff peaks form.

5. Place the whipped cream into a piping bag, then squeeze the whipped cream into the cooled horn molds. Store in the refrigerator until ready to serve.

RELIFE

Ever look at your life and wonder, how did I let it go so wrong? For twenty-seven year old Arata Kaizaki, this thought is a daily occurrence. After quitting his job of three months, claiming it "does not fit his highest potential," Arata has been floundering a bit, trying to get back on his feet. Suddenly unemployable by this action, he is on the verge of being a recluse. Right when he's about to give up, a mysterious man offers him a job opportunity, if he agrees to being part of a scientific experiment. It only entails taking a mysterious pill and enrolling in high school again for a year, but hey, what else does he have to lose?!

Finding himself enrolled in high school life again, I found it touching how hard he tries to help the people around him develop good social relationships. One girl in particular, Chizuru, does not know how to connect with other girls, and always ends up doing more harm than good. In one episode we see the girls talking over lunch, with one girl commenting about how she should really try the omelette rice, a.k.a. omurice, one day. Fast forward a few scenes, and we see Chizuru trying to strike up a conversation about how good the dish is, but alas, the other girls are too caught up in their own drama to notice her! It's hard not to feel for her, but cheer up, the omurice is really good!

OMURICE

Makes 2 servings

CUISINE NOTE: Being relatively quick to make, this dish often appears at the family table, and as such is a popular dish to see in anime. A personal touch is often added by writing something on the top in ketchup. Maybe the person's name, words of encouragement, or even words of anger if a couple is in the middle of a fight!

COOKING TIP: Essentially fancy fried rice, this dish is a great way to use up leftovers. Mix in whatever veggies and meats you need to use up, you really can't go wrong!

Ingredients

- [ ] 4 large eggs
- [ ] ¼ cup cream
- [ ] ⅓ teaspoon salt
- [ ] 1 tablespoon vegetable oil
- [ ] ½ onion, diced
- [ ] 1 clove garlic, minced
- [ ] 1 carrot, diced
- [ ] ¼ cup frozen peas
- [ ] ¼ pound pork, thinly sliced
- [ ] 1 cup cooked rice
- [ ] 2 tablespoons ketchup
- [ ] 1 tablespoon soy sauce
- [ ] Parsley, for garnish

Instructions

1. Combine the eggs, cream, and salt in a small bowl and whisk until well mixed. Set aside.

2. Add the oil to a wide skillet, then add the onions and garlic. Sauté over medium heat until the onions have turned translucent. Add the pork and continue sautéing until the pork has browned.

3. Add carrots and peas to the pan and cook a few minutes more until the carrots have softened. Add the rice, soy sauce, and ketchup, using a spatula to break up any rice clumps. Let cook for a few minutes, until the rice is warmed through.

4. Divide the rice onto two plates, shaping it into a mound, then return the pan to the stove. Pour half the egg mixture into the pan. Spread the egg out evenly, then cover the pan with a lid and turn the heat down to medium low. Let cook for a few minutes, until the egg is just set. Carefully slide the egg on top of one of the mounds, then repeat the process with the remaining egg.

5. Garnish with ketchup and parsley to serve.

HOLMES OF KYOTO

With small, inconsequential mysteries peppered in amongst the day to day operations of a small town shop, the series gives off a unique slice of life feel that draws you in for more. High school student Aoi faces one of the hardest things a young girl can go through, moving in the middle of high school! In an attempt to gain some quick cash to make it back to her friends, she finds herself at an antique shop where she meets a man whose nickname is Holmes. Nicknamed "Holmes" for his deductive skills, Yagashira Kiyotaka, provides her a job that might help her more than she knows.

As the pair work together, a natural friendship blossoms, which is always a treat to watch unfold! While he helps her in the shop, he also helps her in her life, and at one point finds himself visiting her home. Of course, Aoi's mother provides him with snacks, and what better snack to make than apple pie! While this might not quite be an apple pie, these custard filled tarts are a delight to eat, and dare I say, better than mom used to make!

APPLE CUSTARD TARTS

Makes 8 servings

CUISINE NOTE: Widespread apple cultivation in Japan started in the late 1800s, with it now being one of the most enjoyed fruits in the nation. The popular Fuji apple is actually a cross between two American varieties!

COOKING TIP: You can always make your own layered pastry dough by hand, but it can be difficult to get the layers just so. Using puff pastry sheets is a convenient way to get bakery level results without working in a bakery!

Ingredients

- 2 sheets frozen puff pastry
- 1 large apple
- 2 tablespoons butter, divided
- ½ cup sugar, divided
- ¼ cup sake
- ½ teaspoon cinnamon
- 2 eggs, yolks separated from the whites
- 2 tablespoons flour
- 1 cup milk

Instructions

1. Preheat oven to 400 degrees Fahrenheit and line a rimmed baking sheet with parchment paper. Set the puff pastry sheet out to thaw on the counter.

2. Prepare the custard filling by combining the egg yolks and ¼ cup sugar in a small saucepan over low heat. Stir to combine, then add the flour. Gradually add in the milk, stirring constantly until just thickened. Add 1 tablespoon butter, and once melted, remove from heat and let cool.

3. Prep the apple filling by peeling the apple, removing the core, chopping into small cubes. In a separate saucepan, melt the remaining butter over medium heat and add the apple, sake, cinnamon and remaining sugar. Cook for 10–15 minutes, stirring occasionally, until the apple is tender and most of the liquid is evaporated. Remove from heat and let cool.

4. Once the puff pastry has thawed, carefully unfold the sheets and place on a counter dusted with flour. Cut each sheet into 4 squares. Place a spoonful of the apple filling in the middle of the square, followed by a spoonful of the custard. Fold the corner of the square over the filling, pressing opposite corners together to make a triangle. Use a fork to press the edges of the pastry together. Whisk the remaining egg white with water, then brush on top of each pastry.

5. Bake at 400 degrees Fahrenheit for 15 minutes, or until golden brown. Let cool briefly before serving.

FREE! – IWATOBI SWIM CLUB

Haruka Nanase, a.k.a. Haru, has always loved swimming. His elementary school days were filled with swimming with his best friends, but as time passed, the group fell apart. Come high school, Haru finds himself living an uneventful life, wondering how to get motivated and inspired again. When he suddenly encounters his childhood rival Rin, a spontaneous race in the pool makes him realize just how strong Rin has become. What happened?! This shock to his system was just the thing to kick Haru into gear, and soon enough, he's back in the pool. With Rin going to a different school now, they may not be teammates, but all Haru wants to do is swim with his friends, and with good friends by his side, they all make each other stronger.

Like many anime series, while it is a sports story, the emphasis isn't on the sport itself, but on the relationships the sport brings about. We get to see the dynamics of youthful friendships, pushing each other and challenging each other as they all try to achieve their dreams. The sport sets the stage, but the story is told through the little things, such as Haru's favorite food. Throughout the series, grilled mackerel is a staple in his life, as is evident in the fact that his only requirements for an apartment in Tokyo was a roomy bathtub and a grill he can cook mackerel on. Given how easy, delicious, and nutritious mackerel is, that requirement is completely understandable!

SALT GRILLED MACKEREL (SHIOYAKI)

Makes 4 servings

CUISINE NOTE: Due to its simple nature, *shioyaki*, meaning salt grilled, is a great basic recipe to add to your repertoire. Served alongside a bowl of rice, miso soup, and 2 to 3 small sides makes for a classic Japanese style meal, especially for breakfast.

COOKING TIP: Using sake isn't a requirement, but it's useful for several reasons. The obvious one is it adds a little flavor, but it also tenderizes the fish, removes some of the fishy smell, and makes the texture a little plumper. It's a good first step to do anytime you're cooking with fish.

Ingredients

- ☐ 4 mackerel fillets, or other white fish
- ☐ 3 tablespoons sake
- ☐ 2 teaspoons salt
- ☐ 1 lemon, cut into wedges
- ☐ 1 tablespoon oil

Instructions

1. Set the fillets in a shallow pan and pour the sake over them, coating all sides evenly. Let sit in the fridge for 15 minutes.

2. Preheat the oven to 400 degrees Fahrenheit. Remove the fish from the fridge and pat dry with paper towels. Sprinkle them evenly on all sides with salt, then let them sit on the counter for at least 20 minutes while the oven warms up.

3. When ready to bake, pat dry the fillets with paper towels again, removing any excess moisture the salt pulled out onto the surface. Line a baking pan with parchment paper, then place the fillets skin side down and bake for 20 minutes.

4. Once the skin turns golden and crispy, it's ready to eat! Remove from oven and transfer to plates. Serve with a lemon wedge to drizzle over the top for added flavor.

DRAMA

Crafted with emotions in mind, whether they reflect your inner self or heat up your passions!

Drama is a genre that needs no introduction! A quick Google search for Japanese drama will lead you to the juicy storylines we love in several mediums: live action TV shows, films, as well, anime and manga, some titles so popular they have a rendition for them all. While the guilty pleasure to watch is romantic drama, we see elements of drama in all sorts of context. Given that it's very Japanese to emphasize emotions more so than story sometimes in a story, the genre spans all sorts of context, from psychological thrillers and world apocalyptic situations to everyday coming of age stories.

Given that drama can be emotionally heavy, a successful drama is often achieved by blending in action and comedy to lighten the mood. By doing so, it shifts the storyline to be a bit more appealing, drawing in a wide variety of people just looking for a good story. For intriguing types of drama, successful titles include Future Diary, with its deadly survival game and Erased, an unusual murder mystery. For heart wrenching romantic drama, turn to Clannad and Anohana, both beautiful love stories with unexpected hurdles to overcome.

A DRAMATIC DELIGHT

Drama is a dish that tugs at the heart, skillfully bringing the viewer close to tears, then raising them back up to perfect bliss. When done right, the palate should feel cleansed and refreshed, otherwise the taste tends to linger and turn bitter.

First, decide on the flavor palette. Excellent choices are melodrama or romantic drama, but throwing in some elements of teen, sports, or historical drama can blend quite well.

While an endearing female lead is popular, a male character can also work quite well, especially if you decide to forgo romance. There should be an air of innocence about them, perfectly ripe and just on the edge of a personal transformation.

To start, let the character marinate in the seasonings to let flavor slowly develop. When ready, and you'll know when by the feelings it provokes inside you, place over high heat in a pan, developing a nice, strong sear. Not too long, though, to finish, turn the heat down to low and let cook until the meat is fully tender.

Top with some peppery sass or sweet teasing as a garnish and serve.

MARCH COMES IN LIKE A LION

Only in anime could a board game be so intense! Before watching this series, I had never given shogi, Japanese style chess, much thought. Through this series, though, the viewer discovers a hidden world in Japanese society, watching a young player trying to work his way up the ranks and become a pro, while learning about himself and life in the process. Having become a master player in middle school, Rei Kiriyama has faced enormous pressure in his formative years to maintain his status on top. As a result, he's taken poor care of himself, which serves as a reminder that success isn't always the most important thing. In his high school years, Rei must focus not only on his skills, but also on his relationships, for without the support of friends and family, his dreams will be much harder to reach!

In a pivotal moment where Rei faces off against an older player whose career is on the line, watching them play is quite intense! Should he lose the match and let the older man win, retiring in dignity, or should he win, pushing his own career further? Quite the predicament, and it doesn't help that Rei is considerate of others. But not to worry, after their intense match, they reconcile over a Japanese treat: unagi, or eel! Drinking sake while enjoying unagi, there's no problem that can't be solved!

EEL RICE BOWL (UNA DON)

Makes 4 Servings

CUISINE NOTE: This style of cooking is called kabayaki which entails filleting a long fish, then grilling and brushing with a sweet soy sauce called *tare*.

COOKING TIP: Using flour when cooking fish helps retain the shape of the fillet, and results in a crispier texture. As a bonus, the flour helps thicken the sauce, making it extra flavorful!

Ingredients

- ¼ cup soy sauce
- ¼ cup mirin
- 2 tablespoons sugar
- 2 tablespoons sake
- 2 eel fillets
- Salt and pepper, to taste
- 4 cups cooked Japanese rice

Instructions

1. Preheat the oven to broil setting, 550 degrees Fahrenheit.

2. To make the sauce, combine the mirin and sake in a small pan and bring to a boil over high heat. Turn down heat to medium low, then add sugar and soy sauce and simmer for about 10 minutes until thickened. Once tiny foam starts rising up, you're good! Remove from heat and let cool.

3. Place aluminum foil on a baking sheet and lightly grease with oil. Cut each filet in half, then sprinkle with salt and pepper and arrange on the foil.

4. Broil the fish for 5 minutes, until the top starts to brown. Take the fish out of the oven and brush the sauce on top, then place back in the oven and broil for another minute until the sauce starts to bubble.

5. To serve, divide cooked rice among 4 serving bowls and brush some sauce on top of the rice. Place the unagi on top, brush with extra sauce, and sprinkle with pepper and serve.

ANGEL BEATS

What would you do if you suddenly woke up one day and discovered you were dead? If that wasn't shocking enough, finding out you're stuck in high school, forever, is almost too much to take. Yuzuru Otonashi find himself in just this situation, with no memories of who he was before his untimely death. Here in this purgatory of sorts, these students learn to give up any lingering attachments they still have from life before finally going to their next one. But what is the next life? Nobody really knows. And not knowing, why would they want to go there? Making the best of a bad situation, Yuzuru joins a school organization called the Shinda Sekai Sensen, SSS for short, whose mission is to resist!

Being a high school, the students still engage in a normal high school life. Lessons, clubs, and even a cafeteria. In one scene, mapo tofu is being served for lunch, a spicy Chinese dish popular in Japan. Does taste still work the same in the afterlife? Apparently so, since it's spiciness is readily apparent! Maybe that's just the thing they need to stir their passions enough to let go. At the very least, it's enough to make anyone hungry!

MAPO TOFU

Makes 4 servings

CUISINE NOTE: While Chinese in origin, this dish is really popular in Japan! The key to the heat is doubanjiang, made from fermented soy beans and chili peppers.

COOKING TIP: Silken tofu brings in a wonderfully soft texture, but it's very delicate! To help tofu firm up a little bit, you can place it on a plate to drain beforehand. No pressure or anything is required, water will drain out through gravity. I usually let it sit for 15 minutes.

Ingredients

- ¼ cup soy sauce
- 2 tablespoons doubanjiang (chili bean paste)
- 2 tablespoons mirin
- 1 tablespoon miso
- 1 tablespoons oyster sauce
- 1 tablespoons cornstarch
- 4 tablespoons water
- 2 cloves garlic, minced
- 1 inch ginger, peeled and minced
- 2 green onions, thinly cut
- 14 oz silken tofu, cut into 1 inch cubes
- 1 tablespoon sesame oil
- ½ pound ground pork
- 2 cups cooked Japanese rice

Instructions

1. Combine the chili bean sauce, mirin, miso, oyster sauce, cornstarch and water in a small bowl and set aside.

2. In a large frying pan, heat the oil over medium heat and sauté garlic and ginger. Once fragrant, add the pork, breaking it up with a spatula.

3. When the meat has browned, add the seasoning mixture and stir thoroughly. Bring to a boil, then add the tofu and gently stir, coating the tofu with the sauce.

4. Once the tofu is warmed through, add green onions and stir to combine. Remove from heat and serve with rice.

SAILOR MOON

Usagi Tsukino is your typical eighth grade girl, a little awkward, but endearingly so. One day she stumbles upon a talking cat named Luna, which is already a bit to process, but when Luna tells her that Usagi is destined to be Sailor Moon, "champion of love and justice," and she must search for the fabled Moon Princess, what is she supposed to do?! Luckily she's not tasked with this feat alone, and soon enough discovers other Sailor warriors are in her class to support her. Together they fight to save the world from certain doom brought upon by the Dark Kingdom, though not without a bit of mishaps along the way!

While they are powerful warriors engaged in epic battles and larger than life situations, throughout the story, you also see glimpses of the girls just being girls: going to school, hanging out, pigging out on snacks, which is part of what makes the series so successful. By being relatable, the characters draw you in, inspiring us to achieve more than we think we can. In one scene in particular they are sitting outside eating lunch, enjoying some sandwiches made by Sailor Jupiter. The image is so picturesque, young girls enjoying a picnic in the park, and what better picnic food then sandwiches?!

EGG SALAD SANDWICHES (TAMAGO SANDO)

Makes 4 servings

CUISINE NOTE: Walk into any Japanese convenience store and you will see a delicious assortment of Japanese style sandwiches. There are classics like tuna salad and fried pork cutlets, but you can find other interesting flavors, like yakisoba or even fruit!

COOKING TIP: By adding salt to the onion and letting it sit, water is pulled out, creating a quick pickle. Not only does it change the texture, but it also tones down the pungent onion flavor! I often pickle onions and other vegetables in this way whenever I'm making spreads and salads.

Ingredients

- [ ] 8 slices sandwich bread
- [ ] ¼ small onion, diced
- [ ] 1 teaspoon salt
- [ ] 4 hard boiled eggs, peeled and chopped
- [ ] 1 tablespoons mayonnaise
- [ ] 1 teaspoon mustard
- [ ] ¼ teaspoon pepper
- [ ] ½ teaspoon sugar
- [ ] 4 slices ham
- [ ] 4 leaves lettuce

Instructions

1. Combine the salt and onion in a small bowl and massage the salt into the onion. Let sit for 15 minutes, then gently squeeze out the water from the onion.

2. Combine the onion, eggs, mayo, mustard, pepper, and sugar in a small bowl. Stir to combine.

3. To assemble, place a slice of sandwich bread on a cutting board, then layer lettuce, egg mixture, and ham, placing the egg in the middle to help keep the bread from getting soggy. Place another slice of bread on top, then cut off the crusts. Slice in half and enjoy!

HOKKAIDO MILK BREAD

Makes 1 loaf

CUISINE NOTE: The roux from water and flour at the beginning is called tangzhong. Very popular in Asian bakeries, it helps to make a lighter, fluffier bread when baked.

COOKING TIP: The hardest part with baking bread is waiting for it to rise! If you want to prep ahead of time, you can also cover the dough tightly and place in the fridge overnight to rise instead of on the counter. The cooler temperature helps slow the process, but also the longer time helps develop flavor. When ready to bake, set it out on the counter to warm up for about 15 minutes, then roll it into logs and continue on!

Ingredients

- [ ] ¼ cup water
- [ ] 3 cups bread flour, divided
- [ ] ½ cup half and half, divided
- [ ] 1 ½ teaspoons active dry yeast
- [ ] ¼ cup sugar, divided
- [ ] ¾ teaspoon salt
- [ ] ¼ cup sugar
- [ ] 2 large eggs
- [ ] 2 tablespoons unsalted butter, softened

Instructions

1. In a small saucepan, whisk together ¼ cup of water and ⅛ cup of bread

flour until no lumps remain. Heat the mixture over medium-low heat, stirring constantly. Once it starts to lump together to form a ball, remove from heat and let cool.

2. Meanwhile, warm ¼ cup of the half and half to about 110 degrees Fahrenheit by microwaving for 15 seconds. Stir in the yeast and let sit for 15 minutes.

3. In a large mixing bowl combine the remaining bread flour, salt, and sugar. In a smaller bowl combine the tangzhong, yeast mixture, remaining half and half, and one egg and mix well. Make a well in the dry ingredients and pour in all of the wet ingredients. Stir until the mixture forms a loose dough, then knead for 4–5 minutes, or until the dough forms a semi-smooth ball. The dough will be sticky, embrace the mess! Add a sprinkle of flour as needed to make the dough workable, but resist the urge to add too much. Add the butter to the dough, kneading it in for another 4–5 minutes, or until the dough becomes smooth and elastic.

4. Place the dough in a large bowl and cover with plastic wrap. Place in a warm spot and let rise for about 2 hours, or until doubled.

5. Once the dough is doubled, transfer to a lightly floured surface

and punch it down. Divide it into three equal pieces. Roll each piece into a rectangle, then starting at one of the shorter sides, roll it up into a log. Place neatly together in a greased bread pan, then cover and let rise again for another hour until doubled.

6. Preheat the oven to 350 degrees F. Whisk remaining egg with a tablespoon of water, then brush the egg wash over the dough. Bake for 40 minutes, until golden brown on top. Remove from the oven and cover with a towel to cool slightly, then flip the pan upside down and the loaf should slide right out!

OURAN HIGH SCHOOL HOST CLUB

High school is tough. Being a scholarship student at a ritzy private school is even tougher! For Haruhi Fujioka, she has the added pressure of not being able to afford a uniform, wearing a secondhand boy's uniform instead. With her hair so short, she's mistaken for a boy, and not wanting to create trouble, she goes along with it. But when she breaks a priceless vase, she finds herself working for the schools host club to pay off her debt. How long can she pull off being a boy host and entertaining her female classmates? She can't afford to blow her cover!

One unique thing about Japanese culture from the Western viewpoint are maid cafes (and host cafes), where the server doesn't just serve you, but pampers you as well! You're not only buying food, you're buying their attention. Many people find it a great way to escape the pressures of Japanese society and be treated like royalty for a little while. At Ouran High School, they form a club just for this purpose, giving the girls a chance to relax and enjoy fine sweets and teas. While there are far too many sweets to cover in one book, a classic tea time dessert is a rolled sponge cake. Light and airy, it's hard to resist not eating the whole thing at once!

STRAWBERRY ROLL CAKE

Makes 1 cake

CUISINE NOTE: In general, Japanese pastries are incredibly light and fluffy. Instead of using baking powder and baking soda to create the airiness, Japanese desserts often use a meringue to create the main rising effect. A little bit more effort up front, but so worth it! You can leave the cake plain as I do below, or use food coloring with some of the batter to draw patterns on the parchment paper before pouring in the batter!

COOKING TIP: Beating the egg whites can take forever. It might seem like you're getting nowhere, but be patient, the stiff peaks will come!

Ingredients

- ☐ 4 eggs, separated
- ☐ ¾ cup cake flour
- ☐ ¼ teaspoon cream of tartar
- ☐ ½ teaspoon baking powder
- ☐ ½ cup sugar, separated
- ☐ 2 tablespoons milk
- ☐ 2 cups whipped cream
- ☐ ½ cup strawberries, or other berries

Instructions

1. Preheat the oven to 375 degrees Fahrenheit. Prep the pan by lining a 9" x 13" cake pan with parchment paper.

2. Separate the egg yolks and whites into two bowls. Combine the egg yolks with half the sugar and whisk using a hand or stand mixer for a few minutes until fluffy. Gently fold in the milk, then set aside.

3. Add the remaining sugar and cream of tartar to egg whites, then whisk for about 10 minutes until fluffy and stiff peaks form. Set aside.

4. Use a fine mesh sieve to sift cake flour and baking powder. Using a rubber spatula, gently fold the dry ingredients into the egg yolks. Once combined, add a third of the egg whites to the bowl and fold in until incorporated. Add remaining egg whites and stir to combine, taking care not to stir the batter too much.

5. Pour batter into the lined baking pan, using the spatula to evenly spread the batter across the surface. Pick up the pan and gently drop it onto the counter surface a few times to remove any excess air bubbles.

6. Bake for 13–15 minutes until the top of the cake is lightly browned. Use the parchment paper to gently lift the cake out of the pan and onto the counter. Carefully peel away the parchment paper while still hot, then place another sheet of parchment paper over the top of the cake. Starting on one of the shorter ends, roll the cake up into a cylinder, then wrap with a paper towel and let sit until cooled.

7. When ready to assemble, unroll the cake and spread whipped cream evenly across the surface. If desired, add a few pieces of fruit to the filling. Roll up the cake, then using a sharp knife, cut the ends off the cake to reveal a clean edge. Serve as is, sliced into pieces, adorned with extra whipped cream and fruit as desired. Best enjoyed immediately, but it can be kept in the refrigerator for up to three days.

FRESH WHIPPED CREAM

Makes about 2 cups

Ingredients

- ¾ cup heavy whipping cream
- 1½ tablespoons sugar
- 1 tablespoon flavoring, if desired (matcha, chocolate powder, etc.)

Instructions

1. Combine heavy cream, sugar, and flavoring in a large bowl. Using a hand or stand mixer, beat for about 2 minutes until light and fluffy. It should be firm enough that stiff peaks form when the beater is lifted.

2. Use immediately or store in the refrigerator for up to 3 days.

FRUITS BASKET

Tohru Honda has been living with her grandfather since her parents passed away. Some sudden renovations force them to move out for a bit, and having nowhere else to go, she camps out in a tent! That is, until she finds an unexpected place to crash, the home of popular Yuki Sohma. She quickly discovers that the Sohma family has an unusual secret, they're cursed by the spirits of the Chinese zodiac! Promising to keep their secret, can she take it a step further and help them break their curse forever?

One of the most touching moments happens in a scene between Tohru and Kyo, Yuki's angry but misunderstood cousin. Watching him make a rice ball, she comments, "Someone might be envious of you right now. Someone might be admiring something that you yourself hadn't realized yet. When I think about it, the thought makes me want to try a little bit harder." A wonderful reminder to not judge a book by its cover, for what's on the inside that counts!

ONIGIRI

Makes 4 rice balls

CUISINE NOTE: Wondering what's up with the unique triangle shape? Traditionally, onirigi were shaped to look like Mt. Fuji, since it was a special, spiritual place. The thought was, if you ate triangle shaped rice, it would give you the strength of the gods! But you can make your onigiri in whatever shape is easiest: logs, circles, or even disks.

COOKING TIP: As for fillings, anything goes! I use canned tuna here since it's easy to get, but you can get creative with all sorts of things. You can fill them with flaked salted salmon, various greens seasoned with soy sauce, ground pork, scrambled egg...you get the picture. Or you can simply mix sesame seeds into the rice, or even leave them plain!

Ingredients

- ☐ 1 sheet nori seaweed, cut into 4 strips
- ☐ 2 cups freshly cooked Japanese rice
- ☐ 1 tablespoon salt
- ☐ ¼ cup canned tuna
- ☐ 1 tablespoon mayo
- ☐ 1 teaspoon soy sauce

Instructions

1. To prepare, mix together the tuna, mayo, and soy sauce in a small bowl. Cut the nori sheet into thirds, then cut the strips in half. Place the cooked rice on cutting board and divide into 4 portions. Place the salt in a bowl next to you, along with a bowl filled with water.

2. To assemble, take a portion of rice and flatten it out in a disc shape. Wet your hands, then rub a little salt over your hands to help flavor the rice. Place a spoonful of filling on top of the rice, then carefully scoop up the rice into your hands.

3. Gently cup the rice over the filling, covering the filling completely. Press the spot where the rice came together gently with your fingers to help seal it. Then, firmly press the rice into the desired shape. Fold a strip of nori over the bottom, then set aside and continue with the remaining rice.

4. Alternatively, if shaping them by hand is challenging, try laying a piece of plastic wrap out and placing the rice on top. Continue molding the rice over the filling and shaping as above, wrapping the plastic wrap around the rice and twisting the ends together at the top once it's sealed. Apply pressure to the outside of the plastic wrap to shape, then remove the plastic wrap and cover with nori.

5. Serve at room temperature, or if you need to store until a little later, wrap the onigiri in plastic wrap, then wrap in a thick towel and place in the fridge to help prevent the rice from getting too hard.

MY LITTLE MONSTER

Nicknamed "Dry Ice" by her classmates, Shizuku Mizutani is very focused on her future, ignoring social opportunities in favor of studying and academic excellence. Everything was going smoothly, until the slacker Haru Yoshida gets thrown into the mix. After being absent for a few days, Shizuku is tasked with delivering class printouts to him, who immediately greets her as a friend, whether she likes it or not. While annoyed, she's also touched by Haru's innocence, noticing that his image as a violent and uncontrollable monster is actually just a defense, masking a kind and misunderstood soul. Being misunderstood herself, they're perfect for each other! What could go wrong?!

As their budding relationship develops, their socially awkward tendencies sometimes get in the way. But that won't stop Haru from trying to have fun! What do friends and lovers do? They hang out and eat together, so one way or another, he's going to do it. Instead of going for something cliché, he desperately wants to try something a little different, a monjayaki restaurant. A type of dish where you cook it at the table, monjayaki is just as much an experience as it is a meal. And experiences bring people closer together. No wonder he wants to try it so bad!

SAVORY JAPANESE PANCAKES (MONJAYAKI)

Makes 2 servings

CUISINE NOTE: *Monjayaki* is typically cooked at the table, *teppanyaki* style. If you have a tabletop gas stove or even a pancake griddle, give it a try, but it's perfectly fine to cook it in a wide skillet on the stove.

COOKING TIP: Make the dish your own by adding your own favorite ingredients. Try adding mushrooms, corn, tempura crumbles, tofu, even mochi!

Ingredients

- ☐ 1 cup water
- ☐ ¼ cup Worcestershire Sauce
- ☐ ¾ cup flour
- ☐ 1 cup shredded cabbage
- ☐ 4 slices bacon, chopped
- ☐ 4 shrimp, peeled and deveined, chopped
- ☐ ½ cup shredded carrots
- ☐ 3 green onions, chopped
- ☐ Tonkatsu sauce, for serving
- ☐ Mayonnaise, for serving

Instructions

1. Mix the flour, water, and Worcestershire sauce in a small bowl. In a separate bowl, combine the bacon, shrimp and vegetables.

2. Place a wide skillet or flat grilling pan over medium high heat. Add the solid ingredients and cook for a few minutes, until softened. Use iron spatulas to chop the ingredients up as it cooks.

3. Once the ingredients are cooked, mound them up in a ball in the center of the pan, then create a dome in the middle, forming the shape of a donut. Pour the mixed batter in the middle of the donut and bring to a boil.

4. Once the batter is bubbling, fold the vegetables into the center of the batter and stir gently to combine.

When the batter is halfway cooked, fold the mixture in on itself to mix it up a bit, then let it continue to cook a few minutes more.

5. When the batter is just set but still a little wet, it's ready to eat! Serve alongside mayonnaise and tonkatsu sauce, eating it by scraping it directly off the hot plate.

ANOHANA: THE FLOWER WE SAW THAT DAY

Best friends one moment, strangers the next, Jinta Yadomi and his group of childhood friends grew distant after tragedy split them apart. Each dealing with the death of their friend Menma in their own way, some managed to move on, but Jinta still struggles day to day. Now in high school, he's become the class delinquent, barely even going outside. When he starts to hallucinate seeing Menma again, he writes it off as lingering trauma. But as things start to unfold, he realizes she might not be a hallucination after all, but her actual ghost! She won't leave him in peace until he helps grant her final wish, but just what could that wish be? She can't remember!

Dealing with love and loss is hard enough as it is, having to go through so much so early in life is almost too much to bear! Most of us turn to our parents for love and support, but poor Jinta doesn't even have a mother to comfort him anymore. But while he doesn't have her, he still has his memories of her, and what's more comforting than sweets baked with a mother's love? The envy of all his friends, her raisin filled steamed cakes were always in high demand! These steamed cakes might not taste quite as good, after all, her secret ingredient is love, but they sure come close!

STEAMED CAKES (MUSHI PAN)

Makes 4 servings

CUISINE NOTE: Steamed cakes started to appear in Japanese kitchens after WWII, when there was a surplus of wheat flour in Japan and people needed to come up with ways to use it. Sugar was expensive though, so they were traditionally sweetened with chopped sweet potatoes. Nowadays, you can find cakes in sweet and savory flavors, with cheese and corn being surprisingly delicious!

COOKING TIP: Waited too long to eat it, and now it's turned stale? No problem! You can re-steam it for a minute or so to help moisten it up.

Ingredients

- [ ] ½ cup all-purpose flour
- [ ] 1 teaspoon baking powder
- [ ] ¼ teaspoon salt
- [ ] 3 tablespoons sugar
- [ ] ½ teaspoon vanilla extract
- [ ] 3 tablespoons milk
- [ ] 2 tablespoons vegetable oil
- [ ] 1 egg
- [ ] 1 tablespoon matcha, chocolate, or other powdered flavor, optional
- [ ] ¼ cup chocolate chips, coconut shavings, raisins, etc., optional

Instructions

1. Combine the flour, baking powder, salt, and sugar in a small bowl and mix well. Add the vanilla, milk, vegetable oil, and egg and stir until well blended. If using additional flavoring, add in, adding an additional tablespoon of milk of the batter seems too thick.

2. To prevent the cakes from falling too flat, place four cupcake liners inside small ceramic ramekins or bowls. Divide the batter between the four liners, sprinkling any additional flavoring on top.

3. To cook, first add a half inch of water to a wide skillet and place over high heat. Wrap the lid in a kitchen towel to help prevent condensation from dropping onto the cakes. When the water boils, add the ramekins to the pan and cover with the lid. Turn heat down to low and let cook for 8 minutes. Remove from the pan and let cool briefly before eating.

USAGI DROP

Daikichi Kawachi is living the typical bachelor life, working a good job but otherwise going with the flow. This carefree lifestyle is too good to last, though, and when his grandfather suddenly passes away, he returns home to pay his respects. The last thing he would expect upon arriving at the house is seeing a little girl, but there she is, his grandfather's illegitimate daughter Rin! An embarrassment to the remaining family, the shy little girl is ostracized by no fault of her own, and Daikichi, angered by their coldness, announces that he will take her in—despite the fact that he has absolutely no prior childcare experience. But hey, if your heart's in the right place, how hard can it be?

How does a bachelor transition into fatherhood? Not smoothly, that's for sure. Taking everything in stride, they soon develop a close relationship, and we see the joys of caring for a child far outweigh and difficulties he may face. In one touching moment, Rin actually tries to take care of him, making an origami kinpira dish for him at school. While paper carrots may be pretty, I think real carrots may be a bit more delicious!

CARROT KINPIRA

Makes 4 servings

CUISINE NOTE: *Kinpira* is a cooking style of stir frying and simmering in a sweetened soy sauce. Traditionally made with carrot and gobo, any type of crunchy root vegetable will work well.

COOKING TIP: To make this dish really authentic, try cutting the carrots by shaving instead. Working on the tip as if you were sharpening a pencil, place the knife about 2 inches from the top and carefully slice it off, rotating the carrot as you cut it to whittle it away.

Ingredients

- 2 large carrots, cut into thin strips
- 2 tablespoons sesame oil
- 1 tablespoon toasted white sesame seeds
- ½ cup dashi
- 2 tablespoons sake
- 1 tablespoon sugar
- 1 tablespoon mirin
- 1 tablespoon soy sauce

Instructions

1. Place oil in a small skillet over medium heat. When hot, add the carrot and sauté for 3–4 minutes, until just softened. Add the liquid ingredients, simmering until the liquid has almost evaporated.

2. Once the sauce turns into a nice glaze, sprinkle sesame seeds on top and serve.

HISTORICAL

The embodiment of Japanese classics from simpler times.

Just like a well done cowboy western, historical anime paints a rosy picture of Japan's feudal past. A smaller genre, but an important one, by keeping Japan's historical tradition in alive, we get an understanding of the factors that shaped Japan into the unique country that it is. Being a small country with a long history, there is a sense of national pride in their cultural story, and it's not uncommon to see elements of Japan's past still around in modern day streets, so watching historical series is a great way to gain exposure to Japanese culture in general. Swift ninja, proud samurai, ruthless dictators, and powerful priests, historical anime blend fantasy with history to memorialize the heroes, big and small.

But of course, historical doesn't have to entail only Japan! European culture, Victorian England in particular, is also a big influence on Japanese youth in general, as seen in the unique street fashion trends in Tokyo. Using other settings outside of Japan allows animators to tell stories with more creativity, giving unique crossovers of East meets West well worth the indulgence. So, if you're interested in learning a little bit while being entertained a lot, take a bite out of some historical classics.

A TASTE OF THE PAST

Start with a proud but humble character, someone embodying the spirit of feudal Japan. Samurai and ninja are tempting choices, being involved in the politics and memorable events of the time, but everyday tenant farmers make for compelling characters too.

As for flavor, use only the purest of ingredients, since with such simple dishes, lower quality ingredients are easy to taste. Look for ingredients that tell a story of their own, sake and soy sauce made the old fashioned way, rice gathered by hand, all the little details that imbue the spirit of the craftsmen in the final product. We want to taste the character of Japan in every bite.

A well braised dish is the perfect embodiment of the time. Combine all the ingredients in a pot and cover, patiently waiting while it simmers over a low flame. While it's cooking, take a moment to breathe in the aroma, and when you can smell the rice paddies, you're nearly there. When the smell of nostalgia fills the air, it's ready to serve! Eat quickly, for before you know it, the dish will be history!

SAMURAI SEVEN

A beautiful retelling of the classic film Seven Samurai, the series follows the struggles of a rural village struggling against bandits. Looking to protect their precious rice, they enlist the help of seven unlikely samurai to defend them as the rice harvest nears. Intense battles, fantastical swordsmanship, budding romance, a heart wrenching underdog story, and most importantly, delicious rice, what more could you want for an anime?!

While the story is fantasized, having futuristic components and robotic characters, the story does a wonderful job conveying the feel of feudal Japan. The characters are created, but the struggle is real! These farmers spend their whole year tending to the fields, and at the end are forced to eat gruel, the valuable rice being offered up to the ruling class. As such, what better way to pay our respects to the farmers of old than to enjoy a great bowl of rice. As Heihachi said, there are seven gods residing in the rice, let's enjoy this blessing properly!

SEAWEED RICE SEASONING (FURIKAKE)

Makes 16 servings

CUISINE NOTE: This recipe mixes together a classic blend of flavors, but there are other varieties of furikake as well. You can find shrimp, salmon, shiso, kimchi, even egg flavored mixes! It may be called rice seasoning, but that doesn't mean you have to stop with rice! Put it on everything for a sprinkle of additional umami flavor. Ramen, yakisoba, miso soup, even straight out of the jar, it's the magic ingredient to an amazing dish!

COOKING TIP: Toasting the sesame may seem like an unnecessary step, but it helps bring out a deeper flavor from the seeds. The moment you start smelling their nutty aroma, you've unlocked hidden flavor potential!

Ingredients

- ¼ cup white sesame seeds
- ¼ cup black sesame seeds
- 1 tablespoon wasabi paste
- 2 sheets nori seaweed
- 1 teaspoon salt
- 1 teaspoon sugar

Instructions

1. Place a small pan on a burner on medium heat. Add the sesame seeds and toast them for about 5 minutes until fragrant, stirring occasionally. Blend in the wasabi paste and cook a few minutes more, drying out the wasabi a bit. Remove from heat and let cool.

2. Cut a nori sheet in half, then cut in half a few more times until you have a bunch of narrow strips. Stack the strips on top of each other and cut the strips into thin shavings.

3. Add the cooled sesame seeds, salt, and sugar to a mortar and pestle or food processor. Mash or blend for a few seconds until the sesame seeds are split open, then transfer to a tightly sealed container to store.

SAMURAI CHAMPLOO

With a funky hip-hop vibe infused into a classical Japan setting, Samurai Champloo is a unique story to two wondering fighters who get mixed up with a girl. Mugen is a free spirited, animalistic warrior with a break dancing like fighting style. Jin is a solemn ronin samurai who wanders the countryside alone. When they suddenly cross paths, a misunderstanding leads them to fight each other, and so their feud begins. When the ditzy waitress Fuu gets them out of hot water with the local magistrate, they agree to set their differences aside and join her search for the samurai who smells like sunflowers. What could possibly go wrong?

Being a waitress at a dumpling restaurant, food is what brings this unlikely combination of people together. Offering Mugen one hundred dumplings to help her with a difficult customer, Fuu sets them on their path as the encounter gets so wildly out of hand. So, what better way to understand their way of life then enjoying the snack that started it all?

SWEET & SALTY RICE DUMPLINGS (MITARASHI DANGO)

Makes 6 servings

CUISINE NOTE: The dumpling itself is a type of mochi, or rice cake. Made from mochiko flour, or glutinous rice flour, they have a sticky, chewy texture that is similar to a super dense marshmallow. There are so many delicious types of mochi, both sweet and savory. This recipe is a personal favorite since it combines the two!

COOKING TIP: While delicious no matter how you serve them, roasting them on an open flame brings more depth to the texture. Similar to roasting marshmallows, the inside stays soft but the outside gets firmed and charred, creating a delightful bite!

Ingredients

- [ ] 1 cup mochiko flour
- [ ] ½ package soft tofu
- [ ] 2 tablespoons cornstarch
- [ ] ½ cup sugar
- [ ] 4 tablespoons soy sauce
- [ ] 1 tablespoon mirin
- [ ] 1 cup water
- [ ] Wooden skewers

Instructions

1. Mix the tofu and mochiko in a small bowl. The dough should be firm but workable. Add a little water as needed until it can roll into a ball. Form into small balls of about 2 tablespoons of dough each.

2. Bring water to a boil in a large pot. Add the balls and boil for 2–3 minutes until the balls rise to the top.

3. Drain and let cool slightly.

4. Prepare the sauce by combining the remaining ingredients in a small pan. Stir to combine the cornstarch, then place over medium high heat. Cook until the sauce starts to boil, stirring continuously, then remove from heat and let cool.

5. Place three dumplings on each skewer. Heat a nonstick frying pan over medium high heat. Once hot, add the skewered dango and cook for 3–4 minutes until lightly browned. Flip the skewers over and brown the other side.

6. Brush skewers generously with the sauce and serve. They are delicious both hot and at room temperature.

RUROUNI KENSHIN

Peace doesn't come easily after a long and bloody civil war. While swords may be outlawed, grudges are hard to let go, and discontent lies deep in the hearts of many Japanese. Many survivors of the revolution await their chance for vengeance, and the government relies on the assassin Kenshin Himura to keep the peace. Haunted by his past, Kenshin gives up the life of "Battousai the Man Slayer" to repent as a lone wanderer. After his travels land him at the Kamiya Dojo for a short stay, Kenshin finds it harder and harder to turn back to his old ways. Has he finally found a home to move on from his dark past, or must he wander forever?!

While he may be a wanderer, a man's still gotta eat! On several occasions, we see Kenshin dining with his friends at a yakiniku (grilling) establishment in town. A great meal to enjoy with friends, you get to cook it yourselves with a hot grill built into the table. Just go easy on the sake, for hot flames and disorderly conduct don't mix well!

JAPANESE STYLE BARBEQUE (YAKINIKU)

Makes 4 Servings

CUISINE NOTE: Yakiniku is typically cooked at the table, making it a family affair. Portable tabletop stoves are quite common in Japanese kitchens, but you can also use camping stove to give it a try! Perfectly seared meat paired with a sweet and tangy sauce, it's a great party meal to pair with sake.

COOKING TIP: Don't have a grill? No worries! You can still get a nice, charred flavor by using an electric griddle, such as a pancake maker, or getting a wide cast iron skillet and cooking on the stove.

Ingredients

- 1 pound thinly sliced well marbled beef
- 1 onion, thinly sliced
- 1 bell pepper, sliced
- 1 zucchini, cut into thick rounds
- 1 carrot, thinly sliced
- Salt and pepper, to taste
- 1 cup yakiniku sauce for dipping

Instructions

1. Preheat your grill, or skillet if cooking on the stove, for a few minutes till it's warm when you hold your hand over the surface. While it's heating up, sprinkle ingredients with salt and pepper.

2. Cover the surface with a bit of sesame oil, then place a few pieces at a time onto the surface so as not to overcrowd the pan and lower temperature. Cook items with similar cooking times together, such as root vegetables with thick slices of meat, needing 2–3 minutes to cook, or peppers and onions with thin slices of meat, needing only 30 seconds to a minute.

3. Once the meat is done cooking, transfer immediately to a serving plate, or eat right off the grill! Dip pieces in yakiniku sauce, sprinkled with sesame seeds or green onion for added flavor.

SPICE AND WOLF

Being a peddler traveling from town to town, Kraft Lawrence has seen more than his share of the world. Longing to open up his own store and settle down, he's worked hard to turn a steady profit, and with just a little more effort, his dream is almost in sight. When he suddenly discovers a sleeping girl in the back of his wagon, he finds himself with an unexpected traveling partner, a wolf in human form! Holo longs to go back to her home territory, but can't quite remember where it is. Using her wisdom to help increase his profits, the pair make an excellent team, if only she can stop eating her weight in meat!

A common motif in Japanese folktales are wolves and other mystical forest animals being able to take human form. Being a wolf at heart, put meat in front of Holo and it is gone—she'll devour it! At one point in their travels, the pair are cold and hungry, fantasizing about what warm things they'll get to eat when they finally get into town. While they eat a lot of meat dishes, I found it interesting that at that moment, they were craving okoge, or charred rice. While meat dishes may satisfy their hunger, okoge feeds their soul! Served in hot pot, okoge on a cold day is hard to turn down!

OKOGE NABE

Makes 2 servings

CUISINE NOTE: Nabe is the Japanese word for hot pot. A brothy soup with lots of vegetables and thinly sliced meats, it cooks quickly and is often cooked at the table. Serving it in the cooking vessel retains more heat, making it a super satisfying dish for cold winter nights.

COOKING TIP: The thinner the slices, the quicker it cooks! Add in your favorite vegetables and meats, just remember to add the root vegetables first and greens last, since greens take less time to cook.

Ingredients

- 2 cups dashi
- 1 tablespoon sake
- 1 tablespoon sugar
- 2 tablespoons soy sauce
- ½ inch ginger, grated
- 1 teaspoon cornstarch
- 1 cup lightly burnt rice, broken into pieces
- 8 pieces shrimp, peeled and deveined
- 1 carrot, sliced
- ½ cup radishes, sliced
- ½ head bok choy, sliced

Instructions

1. In a donabe, dutch oven, or other heavy pot, combine the dashi, sake, sugar, soy sauce, and ginger and bring to a simmer. Mix cornstarch with a teaspoon of water in a small bowl to create a slurry, then mix into the broth.

2. Add shrimp, radishes, and carrots and let simmer a few minutes until softened. Add in the cabbage and burnt rice and cook one minute more. Remove from heat and serve immediately.

GOLDEN KAMUI

The war may be over, but the battle has yet begun. Former soldier Sugimoto finds himself in need of large sums of money fast. Following the hype of the Hokkaido Gold Rush, he travels north in hopes of making a fortune, but instead finds himself entangled in a manhunt, gathering tattoos of prison convicts to create a treasure map! Roughing it in the wilderness of Hokkaido is hard enough, fighting against vicious convicts as well, this treasure is not for the weak. He finds himself an unexpected ally in a native Ainu girl, Ashiripa, also interested in the treasure for the sake of her people, and the real treasure hunt begins!

While a good story in itself, this series is really noteworthy in that it sheds light on an indigenous culture little talked about in Japan, let alone abroad. When we think of Japan, we tend to think of mainland Japanese culture, but really the region is home to several cultures under the Yamato ethnic group label. The northern Ainu tribes have had a turbulent history with their southern neighbors for years, dating back to at least the 9th century, yet they get cast to the side when talking about Japanese history. While they aren't mainstream Japanese culture, they still deserve their time to shine! Adding a really addictive story on top of it?! It's a series worth binge watching!

CITATAP STEW

Makes 2 servings

CUISINE NOTE: Ainu cuisine is markedly different than that of mainland Japan in that they don't really enjoy raw meat or preserved foods like miso and soy sauce, which we see in the series a Ashiripa learns to love miso. In that spirit, this dish encompasses a traditional style of soup, called ohaw, with chitatap dumplings mixed in, named after the fun, rhythmic sound the knife makes as it chops up the meat!

COOKING TIP: Without a lot of binder in the mix, these meatballs are a bit delicate, so stir the soup gently as it cooks to prevent crumbling.

Ingredients

- [ ] 2 filets salmon
- [ ] 1 teaspoon salt
- [ ] 1 teaspoon cornstarch
- [ ] 2 cloves garlic, minced
- [ ] 1 leek
- [ ] ¼ cup dried shiitake mushrooms
- [ ] 1 tablespoon miso
- [ ] 2 cups dashi

Instructions

1. Place the mushrooms in a small bowl with a cup of water. Let sit for about 15 minutes, until reconstituted.

2. Using a sharp knife, remove the skin off the salmon filets, then roughly chop the filets into chunks. To break the chunks down further, rhythmically start chopping them up with the knife, creating a "tap tap tap" sound against the cutting board. After a minute or so, you should have a rough paste. Place the paste in a small bowl.

3. Finely slice the white part of the leek, then cut the green part into larger chunks. Set aside the green parts, then add the white parts to the salmon paste, along with the cornstarch and garlic. Mix to combine, then shape into meatballs, taking a spoonful at a time and forming it with your hands.

4. Add the dashi to a small pot over medium high heat, along with the mushrooms and their soaking water. Once boiling, add the meatballs in one at a time and let simmer for 5 minutes. Add the remaining leek and simmer 2 minutes more.

5. Just before serving, mix the miso paste with 2 tablespoons of water until diluted, then pour into the pot. Stir to combine, then right before it starts to boil, remove from heat and serve.

GINTAMA

A story that is hard to describe, Gintama is one part historical Tokyo, one part futuristic aliens, one part comedic relief, and one part just silly absurdity! In a world where aliens have invaded Japan, humans have become almost second class, having to set aside their swords to be submissive. One man however, still carries the samurai spirit, and with a touch of recklessness, Gintoki and his friends take on any odd job they can get to pay the bills. And odd jobs they are!

It's a running joke in the series that Kagura is always munching on sukonbu, a jerky like snack made of seaweed. A difficult snack to come across, and an acquired taste at that, these nori strips are just as snackable, but much more accessible. And being relatively low in calories, it's ok to snack away!

NORI STRIPS

Makes 2 servings

CUISINE NOTE: Did you know there is a front and back to a nori sheet? The front side is glossier, and should be the side facing out when making sushi. In this recipe, try sandwiching the back sides together, making the exterior surface just a little cleaner looking.

COOKING TIP: Being dark in color, it's hard to tell if nori has been overcooked. A little bit of cooking brings out a nice toasty flavor, but too much and it's ruined. Don't let them sit in the oven too long!

Ingredients

- ⬚ 4 sheets nori seaweed
- ⬚ 1 teaspoon soy sauce
- ⬚ 1 teaspoon sesame seeds
- ⬚ 1 tablespoon oil

Instructions

1. Preheat oven to 350 degrees Fahrenheit.

2. Use a pastry brush to spread the soy sauce over two sheets of nori. Sprinkle on the sesame seeds over the top, then place the other two sheets of nori on top to sandwich them together, using the moisture to stick the sheets together.

3. Use a pastry brush to spread the oil over both sides of the assembled sheets, then cut the sheets into strips. Place on a baking sheet and bake for 3–4 minutes, until the moisture is evaporated. Let cool, then serve immediately or store in an airtight container for up to a week.

HAKUOKI

An example of a popular video game being turned into an anime, the story follows Chizuru Yukimura as she heads to Kyoto to search for her father. Traveling in Edo period Japan, however, isn't always easy! Suddenly she's attacked by some mysterious strangers, and even more suddenly, she's saved by members of the Shinsengumi! Not quite sure what to make of her, they take Chizuru into custody, but once they learn that her father is the doctor they are also searching for, they decide to keep her around and aid in the search. Chizuru's father was rumored to have created a magical elixir that increases speed, strength and healing abilities, so naturally everyone is trying to get their hands on it. Can they find her father before the strange men, and what exactly have they stumbled into?

When Chizuru first encounters the Shinsengumi, they aren't sure what to make of each other. While they have a common enemy, that's not enough to make them friends. But given that they risked their lives to save her, she feels a sense of indebtedness to them; after all, they did not come out unscathed. What can she do to bridge the gap? A peace offering of food! A hearty bowl of miso soup, coming right up!

CLASSIC MISO SOUP

Makes 4 servings

CUISINE NOTE: Miso soup really only needs one ingredient, miso! Japanese cuisine tends to celebrate the seasons, so it's common to vary the ingredients depending on what's freshest at the time. Carrots, potatoes, fish, mushrooms, spinach, etc.

COOKING TIP: Don't let it boil! Just simmer it as hot as you want it to be, otherwise the miso will turn grainy.

Ingredients:

- 4 cups dashi
- ¼ cup white miso paste
- 1 block tofu, drained and cut into ½ inch cubes
- 4 green onions, chopped

Instructions

1. Place the dashi in a small pot over high heat. Once boiling, turn the heat down and add the tofu.

2. Ladle out a spoonful of dashi and place in a small bowl. Add the miso and stir until it has fully dissolved into a thinner paste. If needed, add a little more dashi until it will pour easily, then add back to the pot.

3. Let simmer until the tofu has warmed through, then add the green onion and transfer to bowls to serve.

DESCENDING STORIES: SHOWA GENROKU RAKUGO SHINJU

Before film and TV, radio and stage reigned supreme. But it wasn't just music and acting; stand-up comedy, or rakugo, were accessible to all, on stage and over the radio. Enamored by the famous Yakumo's rendition of the classic rakugo story "Shinigami," a young man wants nothing more than to be his apprentice upon his release from prison. Yakumo accepts him, appointing him the new name "Yotaro." But the path to Rakugo fame isn't easy, and his determination is put to the test as he struggles to master the subtleties of the art.

For a story about comedians, this story is surprisingly sad! A beautiful example of Japanese outlook on life, living is challenging, but that struggle and sadness can be quite beautiful. Love, loss, and tragedy are everywhere, but happiness can be found where you least expect it. In one scene we see a young girl performing her own rakugo for patrons at a soba shop, just trying to make a buck. While her comedy might not be for everyone, a good bowl of noodles is hard to turn down!

CHILLED SOBA

Makes 1 serving

CUISINE NOTE: Traditionally chilled soba is served on a bamboo tray. Visually appealing, it's also practical, since it prevents the noodles from getting soggy as it sits on a plate's surface.

COOKING TIP: You may be wondering why the noodles are served alongside a separate dipping sauce. Enjoying it this way ensures the noodles don't get excessively soggy, maintaining a firm, chewy texture throughout your meal!

Ingredients

- [ ] 1 cup dashi
- [ ] ⅓ cup soy sauce
- [ ] ⅓ cup mirin
- [ ] 1 teaspoon sugar
- [ ] 1 bundle dried soba noodles
- [ ] ½ teaspoon wasabi, or to taste
- [ ] 1 green onion, finely chopped
- [ ] 1 large sheet nori, cut into thin strips

Instructions

1. To make the broth, bring dashi, soy sauce, mirin, and sugar to a boil over medium heat. Immediately remove from heat and let cool.

2. To prepare the noodles, bring a small pot of water to boil over high heat. Once boiling, add soba and cook the noodles until just softened, about 3–5 minutes. Once cooked, immediately transfer to a mesh strainer and place under a running faucet to cool the noodles down.

3. To serve, drain the noodles thoroughly and place in a mound on a small place. Mix the wasabi and green onion into a small bowl combined with the prepared dipping sauce. To eat, dip the noodles in the sauce before each bite to prevent the noodles from becoming soggy.

POST-CREDITS

Ever stick around at the end of the movie to read the credits? Most Americans would say no, the movie is over, so why stick around? In Japan, on the other hand, leaving before the credits finish rolling is seen as rude! It's only right to sit till the very end and show your respect to the filmmakers. Western filmmakers sometimes reward the audience for making it to the end with a bonus scene, so to reward you for making it this far, we've saved the best for last! A Japanese treat loved by all: pocky!

HOMEMADE POCKY

Makes 16 servings

CUISINE NOTE: Made by Glico since 1966, pocky is loved all over the world and is easily one of the most recognizable Japanese snacks. Named after the sound it makes as you snap the stick in two, it comes in all sorts of flavors, the classics being chocolate and strawberry.

COOKING TIP: Chocolate can be temperamental as it cools! It may be easier to work with smaller batches of chocolate at a time, just in case it starts to get unworkable.

Ingredients

- 1¼ cups all-purpose flour
- 1 tablespoon sugar
- ¼ teaspoon salt
- ¼ cup unsalted butter
- 3 tablespoons milk
- ¼ teaspoon almond extract
- 1 cup chocolate chips
- ¼ crushed almonds

Instructions

1. Combine all dry ingredients into a food processor and pulse one or two times. Cut the butter into small chunks and add in, along with the milk and almond extract. Pulse a few more times until it's well crumbled, then place onto a lightly floured surface and press the dough together until a ball forms. Wrap the dough with plastic wrap and leave it in the fridge for 30 minutes.

2. When the dough is chilled, preheat the oven to 350 degrees Fahrenheit. Place the dough on a lightly floured surface, then roll it out until it's about a ¼ inch thick.

3. Form the dough into a rectangle shape, cutting off excess dough on the sides. Then cut it into thin strips about ¼ inch wide.

4. Place the strips on a baking sheet lined with baking paper and bake in the oven for 18–20 minutes. Once lightly browned, remove from oven and transfer to a wire rack to cool.

5. Meanwhile, prepare the toppings by first roughly chopping the almonds with a knife and transferring to a wide plate. Melt the chocolate by placing them in a microwave safe bowl. Microwave them for 30 seconds at a time, stirring in between each time, and stop just when the chocolate gets warm enough to melt.

6. Working quickly to keep the chocolate at a warm temperature, dip each stick the melted chocolate, then give a quick tap on top of the crushed almonds to coat each stick. Transfer to wire rack to cool.

7. Once the chocolate is set, enjoy immediately or store in an airtight container.

ACKNOWLEDGEMENTS

To all the people who made this silly little dream of mine into a reality, thank you! My husband, for unwavering support and enthusiasm for all my crazy ideas; my parents, for believing in me and nourishing my potential; my family and friends, for their feedback and critiques; Mango Publishing for giving me a platform to share my voice; and to all of you, dear readers, for your interest in my work. You all are amazing!

ABOUT THE AUTHOR

A self proclaimed Japanophile, Danielle Baghernejad has spent much of her life exploring the many aspects of Japanese culture. Her dream of experiencing the nuances of Japanese cuisine firsthand came true after an appearance on the Japanese TV show, *Sekai! Nippon Ni Ikitai Hito Ouendan.* Since then, she has worked to make authentic Japanese recipes more available to a Western audience. A ceramicist by day with Zenful Pottery, a foodie by night with OtakuFood.com, she spends her spare time in the kitchen tying her two loves together with her husband Eamon and daughter Giselle.

Printed in the USA
CPSIA information can be obtained
at www.ICGtesting.com
JSHW071423290424
62133JS00021B/438

9 781642 503333